THE
GUIDE
TO THE
FEDERAL
BUDGET

THE
GUIDE
TO THE
FEDERAL
BUDGET

Fiscal 1984 Edition

STANLEY E. COLLENDER

An Urban Institute Paperback

THE URBAN INSTITUTE PRESS · WASHINGTON, D.C.

CARR

LC 82-643840
ISSN 0730-9511
ISBN 0-87766-321-1
Please refer to URI 34700 when ordering

Printed in the United States of America

HJ
2050
.C6
South
A
5L
1. Budget - United States.
2. Fiscal Policy - United States.
I. Title.

CONTENTS

FOREWORD

For an issue as widely discussed and debated during the past two years as the federal budget, there is a woeful lack of understanding about the process and the method of "budget making." Part of the reason for this lack of understanding stems from the fact that a "budget" is not just a set of cold numbers. Instead, a budget embodies the hopes and goals for our nation.

This lack of understanding may come as a shock to people who assume that the enormous amount of publicity and activity on "the budget" during 1981 and 1982 makes any guide to the process superfluous. Indeed, in the 97th Congress, we did spend a large amount of our time grappling with budget-related issues, and extensive space was devoted to our work by the written and electronic media.

Unfortunately, the coverage of the "budget" numbers has tended to obscure the process, and to even shy away from the very important substantive issues. Instead, for the past two years, we have seen the discourse on the budget revolve around a super "sporting event" theme. The question has rarely been asked: "What is the best economic policy for our nation and our citizens?" The attention has not centered on the reality of those policies; instead, the focus has been on confrontation revolving around the questions, "Who is on first base?"; "Will the administration get everything it wants?"; and "Is Congress going to defeat the president's proposals?"

In such a climate, it is no wonder that the process has received short shrift. The irony, of course, is that this ignorance persists at the very time the budget process is being called upon to do more and more. In fact, it was almost destroyed by the pressures of budget making in 1981. The majority of Congress chose to ignore the procedural constraints that year, and instead focused solely on putting in place a set

ix

of policies that made fundamental changes in our federal government. Some of these changes appear to be good, some of them are demonstrably bad. Taken as a whole, they have left us with enormous economic problems that will further tax the process in the coming years.

A year ago, some observers doubted that the budget process could survive. That view no longer holds much sway because a majority of Congress concluded that the procedural excesses of 1981 must not be allowed to happen again. By returning to the use of the process in a fair and constructive manner, Congress and the nation have a chance to confront our very real economic problems in a responsible fashion.

All of us know that solving those problems will not be easy. The current system has worked. The timetable and provisions of the Budget Act make sense. With that said, we must understand that while the budget process can help us, it alone cannot save us, nor can it make the difficult choices for us that lie ahead. The process is no substitute for the hard political decisions we face, but by using it correctly, we can move decisions forward for debate and disposition.

As a beginning, then, decision makers, those who seek to shape policy, and the general public must understand the Budget Act. This volume does an outstanding job of beginning that educational task, and it is my pleasure to provide this foreword to the very fascinating and also very frustrating congressional budget process.

James Jones
Chairman, Committee on the Budget
U.S. House of Representatives

PREFACE

Even though it passed unanimously in the Senate, and with only six opposing votes in the House, there was much doubt about the survival of the new congressional budget process after it was created in 1974. Indeed, because the process was perceived to be so fragile, many of the early activities connected with its implementation were designed to support and sustain it. The determination of national priorities and fiscal policy was considered secondary.

Much initial skepticism was justified because the new process seemed to commit the ultimate congressional sin of infringing on the jurisdiction of other committees. The only previous attempt by Congress to impose a budget process on itself failed in 1949, a scant three years after it was created.

It is now obvious, however, that the process has not only survived but grown steadily in importance. The Budget Committees in both the House and the Senate are moving confidently, even boldly, to impose the process on all congressional activities. Many of these activities are now clearly subordinate to the procedures the Budget Act established. Even the executive branch has come to realize the significance of the congressional budget process, and the Reagan administration has used it in imaginative new ways to impose its own economic program. In fact, the president probably would not have been as successful in achieving the dramatic changes he has proposed had it not been for the reconciliation provisions of the Budget Act; the attention this process focuses on the budget debate; Congress's ability to determine fiscal policy and spending targets in the first concurrent budget resolution; and the increased budget and economic sophistication of members of the House and Senate. These occurrences are a direct result of the implementation of the budget process.

Ironically, it has been Ronald Reagan's actions that have inadvertently given the process the final push needed to establish its credentials firmly both in Congress and in the public's eye. This is so because of the extraordinary spending reductions the president has proposed. Before the Reagan administration came into office, the budget process provided few real spending constraints since the targets and ceilings of the budget resolutions usually left ample room for the authorizing committees and Appropriations Committees to act. Thus, the most significant decisions were reserved for these committees, and interest groups and lobbyists were forced to concentrate on this traditionally important phase. Reagan's cutbacks, however, severely limited the choices of these committees and made their actions somewhat less important than those of the Budget Committees, which drafted the resolutions to which the authorizing committees and Appropriations Committees had to conform. This was especially true for the authorizing committees, which were issued specific instructions in the bill. The Appropriations Committees were also affected. These committees could not provide more money for a program than had been authorized. The fact that in some circumstances the Budget Committees could be given the authority to recommend the necessary cuts if the authorizing committees refused to comply with the reconciliation instructions was another indication that the budget process had greatly changed the way Congress was conducting its affairs.

Recent experiences have demonstrated that the budget process no longer is solving all the problems that it was designed to solve. The process has even created several new problems. The most obvious failure has been keeping Congress on schedule. At the start of fiscal year 1983 on October 1, 1982, Congress had passed only three appropriations bills in final form. For the third consecutive year, the federal government was operating on a continuing resolution. The budget process has also produced new opportunities for presidential-congressional confrontations. In 1982 this included a dramatic and lengthy stalemate between the two branches of government that seriously delayed all budget activities for many months.

With the deep spending cuts proposed in the fiscal 1982 and 1983 budgets and the strong possibility of more cuts in the coming years—and, therefore, the realization that the experiences with recent budgets are typical of how Congress will act in the future—there seems to be a real change in attitude toward the congressional budget process. Many of those who have avoided the subject now realize that failure to consider the provisions of, and most recent changes in, the budget process can jeopardize the chance for successful enactment of legislative programs. Washington veterans, both on and off Capitol Hill, as well as those who view the events at some distance, look attentively at the budget process. Congressional scholars, who until now have looked at the budget reform as only a temporary variation, now see it as a permanent change in the legislative process and want to include it in their analyses of House and Senate actions. In other words, the budget process has not only been implemented; it has been accepted.

This book is not an analysis of the fiscal 1984 budget proposed by President Ronald Reagan. It is not an historical account of how the budget process came into being or evolved into its current form. Many other sources provide this information, and there is no need to duplicate them.

Instead, this book is intended to fill the one gap left by other works. This book is a practical guide to the congressional budget process and the federal budget. To enhance its usefulness, this guide is based on the current budget proposal and the steps that will determine it. The book describes those steps, explains their significance, details the procedures under which they will probably take place, identifies steps that may fall by the wayside, and lists the important decision makers involved in each stage. This guide also explains how to read and use the fiscal 1984 budget, including the first complete description of each of the five major budget documents submitted by the president to Congress. All of the budget figures discussed, tables used as examples, and page numbers cited as references are from the presidential budget proposal for fiscal 1984, which Congress now is debating.

This "cookbook" approach enables readers to use the information for their own purposes, regardless of their substantive interest or political ideology. It can serve both as a primer for those who need to learn the process or budget in toto, or as a quick-reference guide for those who want to check a particular point. For individuals who only recently have recognized the budget and budget process as being important, this book will serve as the fastest means of developing the knowledge necessary to work with them.

That this book exists at all is the result of the efforts of a number of people who have taken the time in the past to criticize, encourage, inspire, or otherwise work with me. For some, like Aaron Wildavsky, my former dean at the Graduate School of Public Policy of the University of California, Berkeley, and the author of *The Politics of the Budgetary Process*, the debt is largely intellectual. He will never know how challenged I feel by his constant questions and by my desire to live up to the standards he has set with his work. For others, like Mace Broide, Robert Giaimo, Robert Hartman, and Robert Reischauer, the debt is more direct because of my association with them over the past few years and their willingness to listen to and comment on my ideas and schemes. I am grateful to them also for reviewing this book in one or more of its earlier versions. Similarly, I would like to thank Wendell Belew, Michelle Flotteron, Bill Hagan, David Klaus, Bruce Meredith, John Nelson, and Deidre Reimer, who also read part or all of earlier drafts.

I owe a very special thanks to the staff of the Urban Institute Press, whose dedication and professionalism are only matched by their good cheer. I am especially grateful to Shaun Murphy for her confidence in me and the project, and to Theresa Walker for curing me of my fear of editors.

As with the fiscal 1983 edition, some of the best help I received had nothing to do with the budget. I would not have been able to complete this project had it not been for the repeatedly tested ability of Jim Dowaliby, Barbara Geller, and Bruce Leffler, to calm me down at odd hours of the day and night, not to mention their willingness to go for Chinese food at the slightest provocation. Susan Bales deserves mention because of her extraordinary abilities and hard work to make the book better known. Finally, I again want to acknowledge the contribution of my Wednesday breakfast companions, Mark Bodden, Steven Brown, Gary Conkling, Tom Cowley, George Kundanis, and Sara Sibley.

This book is dedicated to Maura McGinn for her constant support and many, many smiles.

Stanley E. Collender
Washington, D.C.

INTRODUCTION

One has had to live through the topsy-turvy political world of 1981 and 1982 to believe what has occurred. An imaginary dialogue may do some justice to the situation.

Liberals: How dare President Reagan unbalance the budget, thus causing the perpetuation of high interest rates!

Conservatives: Why are you so rigid?

Liberals: Men may be wrong but the market is right. Listen to the market!

Conservatives: What does Wall Street know?

What, indeed, does anyone know about budgeting anymore? The eternal verities, the product of centuries of hard-won reform—budgetary comprehensiveness, budgetary balance, and budgetary annularity—are under severe strain. The annual budget, seemingly forever a fixture of modern government, may well be replaced by a biennial budget. There is just too much work done too hurriedly and too late to justify doing it all so often. Besides, with perspectives shifting so radically that budgets are made and remade every few months, one year appears too long as long as well as too short. The norm of comprehensiveness can hardly withstand the variety of spending spigots—direct loans, guaranteed loans, off-budget corporations, entitlements, tax expenditures, tax credits, on and on—and the multitudinous purposes they are supposed to serve. Maybe, after all, the old-fashioned appropriation really is not comparable to all the other sources of spending. As for balance, it does matter whether the deficit is incurred through higher spending or lower taxing. Would the reader prefer a $700 billion budget with a $100 billion deficit or a $900 billion budget with a $50 billion deficit? Is it the size of the deficit or the size of government that matters most? The answer, whatever it is, involves far more than economic theory, even if there were agreement on the consequences of a deficit, which plainly there is not.

Nowadays, budgeteers speak in strange tongues, that is, reconciliation refers to conflict. The learned doctors mumble about first and second resolutions: What would happen if the last become first? That depends. The Congressional Budget and Impoundment Control Act of 1974 did not decree lower spending, nor did it alter political incentives one whit. What the act did do was change calculations so that Congress could work its will, whatever that was, more effectively. The purpose of the second resolution, as I know from discussion at the time, was to legitimize budgeting by addition by formalizing the usual congressional tendency to lump together its item-by-item decisions and call them a budget, much as presidents do when the document has to be sent to the printer. Making the first resolution binding might signify a desire to introduce budgeting by subtraction (or resource allocation, as the old-fashioned phrase had it), through which agencies and programs compete under a fixed total. It might but it might not. For the tendency might be to agree on so high a limit that it would not be difficult to include new spending. The result of making the first resolution all-important in principle would then be to trivialize it in practice. Only if the first resolution were to bite by being not too far from where we are now would it matter. And that would be a far bigger change than anyone (except the Canadians, who by cabinet resolution have tied spending increases to the growth of their national product) has yet contemplated.

In the midst of all this flux it is good to have Stan Collender's expert account of how the existing budget process works. Life has moved so much faster than observation that this is the first extended effort to describe the steps in the budgetary process circa 1981–1983. Since this book will be supplemented by a newsletter, readers should buy big binders. From the novice to the afficionado, practitioners and students of budgeting are in the author's debt for fixing the first benchmark in American federal budgeting of the new era.

Aaron Wildavsky
University of California, Berkeley

ABOUT THE AUTHOR

Stanley E. Collender is president of The Budget Research Group, Inc., a Washington-based consulting organization that specializes in the federal budget and congressional budget process. He is also the publisher of *Federal Budget Report*, the only newsletter devoted entirely to presidential and congressional budget activities.

Mr. Collender is one of only three people to have worked for both the House and Senate Budget Committees. He has been involved with the congressional budget process since its inception in 1974. As a member of the House Budget Committee staff he served as administrator of the Task Force on State and Local Government; for the Senate Budget Committee he was responsible for analyzing defense spending. Mr. Collender also served as administrator of the Task Force on the Budget of the Northeast-Midwest Congressional Coalition, a bipartisan group of over 200 members from the eighteen states in those regions.

Mr. Collender's experience includes service on the legislative staffs of Representatives Fortney H. Stark, Jr., and Elizabeth Holtzman. He also served as administrative assistant to Representative Thomas J. Downey and to the deputy assistant secretary for health planning in the Department of Health, Education, and Welfare.

Over the past year Mr. Collender has appeared on a number of television and radio programs as an expert on the federal budget. Among the more notable are Good Morning America (ABC), C-SPAN (Cable), Tony Brown's Daybreak (WRC-TV), The Barry Gray Show (WMCA-Radio), and Newsmakers (WINS-Radio).

Mr. Collender holds a master's degree in public policy (MPP) from the University of California, Berkeley, and a B.A. from New York University. He is the author of *The Guide to the Federal Budget, A Step-By-Step Guide to Understanding the Federal Budget*, and numerous articles on the federal budget and congressional budget process.

CHAPTER 1

THE FEDERAL BUDGET AS A SECOND LANGUAGE

Before delving into the congressional budget process, some specialized terms must be explained. The following key terms and concepts should be mastered before even attempting to review the budget process or to analyze individual budget documents. (The glossary will also be helpful in learning the language of the federal budget.)

Authorization vs. Appropriation

Two steps usually must occur before the federal government can spend money on an activity. First, an "authorization" must be passed allowing a program to exist. The authorization is the substantive legislation that establishes the purpose and guidelines for a given activity and usually sets a limit on the amount that can be spent. The authorization does not, however, provide the actual dollars for a program nor does it enable an agency or department to make commitments to spend funds in the future. Second, an appropriation must be passed. The appropriation enables an agency or department to (1) make spending commitments and (2) spend money.

Except in the case of entitlements, an appropriation is the key determinant of how much will be spent on a program. In almost all cases, however, an appropriation for a given activity cannot be made unless and until the authorization is passed. No money can be spent on a program unless it first has been allowed (authorized) to exist. Conversely, if a program is authorized but no money is provided (appropriated) for its implementation, that activity cannot be carried out. Therefore, both an authorization and an appropriation are necessary for an activity to be included in the budget.[1]

A particularly confusing aspect of these two legislative requirements is that both authorizations and appropriations describe an ac-

1

tivity in dollar terms. For example, the authorization for the administrative expenses of the United States Railway Association (USRA) for fiscal 1982 (Public Law 97-35) stated as follows:

> There are authorized to be appropriated to the Association for purposes of carrying out its administrative expenses under this Act not to exceed $13,000,000 for the fiscal year ending September 30, 1982. . .

While the fiscal 1982 appropriation (Public Law 97-102) for USRA stated as follows:

> For necessary administrative expenses to enable the United States Railway Association to carry out its functions under the Regional Rail Reorganization Act of 1973, as amended, $13,000,000, to remain available until expended, of which not to exceed $1,000 may be available for official reception and representation expenses.

Despite the fact that both seem to be providing funds, only the appropriation actually is doing so. The dollar figures in the authorization serve only as an upper limit on what can be appropriated. An appropriation never can exceed the authorization for the same program.

An "entitlement" is a particular type of authorization. Entitlement legislation requires the federal government to pay benefits to any person or unit of government that meets the eligibility requirements it establishes. Although an entitlement requires an appropriation before funds can be spent, it differs from other authorizations because it constitutes a legally binding commitment on the federal government. In fact, eligible recipients may sue for their benefits if such benefits are denied because money is not appropriated. The authorization is the key legislation in deciding how much will be spent on an entitlement and relegates the appropriation to little more than a formality. Examples of entitlement programs are Medicaid, Medicare, and Social Security.

Budget Authority vs. Outlays

The dollar amounts listed in both authorization and appropriation bills are stated in terms of "budget authority."

Budget authority (BA) is the permission granted to an agency or department to make commitments to spend money. This includes hiring workers (committing funds for salaries) and signing contracts to procure some items (committing funds for payment upon completion of the contract). In most cases, budget authority is not the level at which a program will function but is merely the level of new spending commitments that will be or have been made. It is important to remember that although budget authority will lead to the spending of money, it is not the actual exchange of cash.

Outlays (O), on the other hand, are the actual dollars that either have been or will be spent on a particular activity. Outlays are the direct result of budget authority, that is, of commitments to spend money made either this year or in previous years. The level of outlays is the key number to use in determining how much has been or will be spent on a program. It is the overall level of outlays compared to the overall level of revenues that determine whether the budget is in surplus or deficit.

Figures for both budget authority and outlays are needed because many government activities cannot be completed within a single fiscal year, and it is important to know both the total cost (budget authority) and what actually will have to be spent this year (outlays). By looking beyond this year's spending requirements to the overall cost of the activity, the president and Congress can know the future spending commitments they are making as well as the cash required immediately.

This is particularly important for activities that take several years to complete, for example, the procurement of an aircraft carrier. In this case outlays in the first year will be relatively small because it takes a long time to start construction. The budget authority in the first year, however, will be large since it will reflect the full cost of the ship. In the second year there will be no new budget authority because the full cost was provided in last year's budget, and the permission to commit funds was granted previously. Outlays for this ship, however, will begin to increase in the second year as construction continues and accelerates. This pattern of no new budget authority but increasing outlays will continue each year until the procurement is completed.

A good analogy to this example is the purchase of an automobile with a three-year loan. When the purchase of the car (at a total cost of $10,000, for example) first is arranged, a contract is signed for the full amount and the "budget authority" is $10,000. But the actual amount to be spent ("outlays") in the first year is equal only to the down payment plus the monthly payments ($5,000). In the second year no new budget authority is needed because the loan already has been arranged and the commitment made, but the outlays are equal to the monthly payments ($2,500 in this case). In the third and final year again there would be no new budget authority, but the outlays again would equal $2,500, at which point the loan would be repaid. Table 1 shows how the federal budget typically depicts this situation.

It should be clear from table 1 that neither budget authority nor outlays is sufficient by itself to tell the full budgetary consequences of purchasing this car. By looking only at budget authority in fiscal 1984, the program might seem too expensive to undertake since the full cost of the car appears to be needed in that year. Yet by looking only at the

TABLE 1
PURCHASE OF AUTOMOBILE (*in thousands of dollars*)

	Fiscal year		
	1984	1985	1986
Budget Authority (BA)	10	0	0
Outlays (O)	5	2.5	2.5

budget authority in fiscal years 1985 or 1986, the car looks too good to pass up since it appears to cost nothing even though substantial spending is, in fact, required. If you look only at the outlays in a particular year, you would not easily know the full cost of the car since only the yearly spending requirements are obvious.

Some governmental activities, notably the payment of salaries and entitlements, usually "spend out" within the fiscal year in which the budget authority first is provided. In these cases budget authority and outlays are approximately equal. In some cases, however, the level of outlays appears to be greater than the level of budget authority. This is the result of budget authority provided in previous years that only now is being spent. The level of outlays for a single year is, therefore, the combination of budget authority provided this year and in previous years.

It is difficult, however, to determine simply by looking at the tables in the budget whether outlays are the result of budget authority provided this year or in previous years; usually some knowledge of the program is necessary. Take the previous example of an automobile purchased with a three-year loan. If another car is purchased in a similar manner at the same cost in fiscal 1985, the budget typically would depict the situation as shown in table 2.

It would be wrong to assume that the $7,500 in outlays in fiscal 1985 is the result of the $10,000 in budget authority provided in fiscal

TABLE 2
PURCHASE OF TWO AUTOMOBILES (*in thousands of dollars*)

	Fiscal year		
	1984	1985	1986
Budget Authority (BA)	10	10	0
Outlays (O)	5	7.5	5

1985. In fact, only $5,000 comes from this new budget authority. The remaining $2,500 comes from budget authority provided in fiscal 1984 that is now coming due (the monthly payments from the automobile purchased in that year). Even if the entire $10,000 in budget authority were cut from the 1985 budget, $2,500 still would be spent in fiscal 1985, since that is the result of previous spending decisions. Fiscal 1986 spending, however, would drop to $2,500.[2]

Figure 1 depicts the relationship between budget authority and outlays in the fiscal 1984 budget as a whole. The president proposed a budget with outlays of $848.5 billion (upper right-hand corner). Only 85.4 percent of that amount or $724.8 billion will result from the fiscal 1984 budget authority of $900.1 billion (upper left-hand corner), however. The remaining 14.6 percent or $123.7 billion will result from unspent budget authority granted in previous years (lower left-hand corner). The $175.3 billion in budget authority to be provided in fiscal 1984 that does not result in fiscal 1984 outlays will be added to the $746.3 billion in budget authority provided in prior years that will continue to remain unspent. This $921.6 billion is the total amount of unspent budget authority that will result in outlays in the future (bottom right-hand corner).[3]

Controllable vs. Uncontrollable

The $921.6 billion in unspent budget authority is a significant part of what is classified as "relatively uncontrollable" spending. Such spending is not out of control in the literal sense. It is the outlays resulting from previous commitments by the federal government. This includes already granted budget authority, entitlements, open-ended programs on which no limit has been placed, which increase automatically as the economy changes, and budget authority provided through permanent appropriations (interest on the national debt, for example), which requires no further action by Congress. Of the $848.5 billion in outlays in the fiscal year 1984 budget submitted by the president, over $654.6 billion or 77.1 percent can be classified as relatively uncontrollable.

"Controllable" spending is spending that will occur only if Congress passes an appropriation for it.

Uncontrollable is, however, a misnomer, since, if Congress chooses to act, it can change any and all existing laws to alter the amount

FIGURE 1
RELATION OF BUDGET AUTHORITY TO OUTLAYS

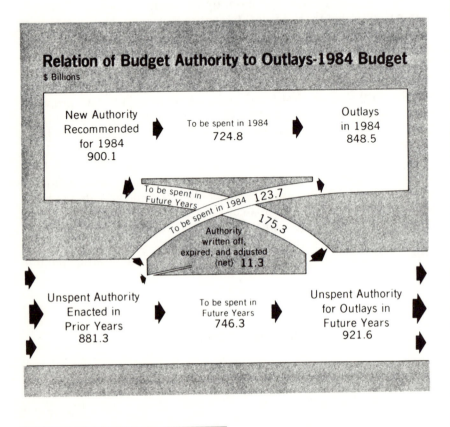

Reprinted from Office of Management and Budget (OMB), Budget of the United States Government, Fiscal Year 1984 (Washington, D.C.: Government Printing Office, 1982), p. 6-5 (hereafter referred to as the Budget).

Note: This and many subsequent tables and figures are reprinted from OMB, Budget of the United States Government, Fiscal Year 1984. In the source shown, the page on which these tables are found in the Budget or in the other budget documents will be cited.

For the reader's convenience, tables and figures are numbered consecutively throughout The Guide to the Federal Budget. Although most tables are not designated by number in OMB's Budget, the table titles do correspond to the table titles printed in The Guide.

expected to be spent or to stop it entirely. In other words, controllable spending will occur only if Congress takes some action to cause it. Uncontrollable spending will occur only if Congress takes no action to stop it.

Economic Assumptions

The federal budget is very sensitive to changes in the economy. The spending level of many programs changes as inflation and unemployment increase or decrease. Similarly, the amount of revenues collected by the government changes if the economy (usually measured by the gross national product [GNP]) is declining or growing since businesses and individuals pay taxes based on their earnings. Whenever the president and Congress formulate the budget they must, therefore, make certain assumptions about how well or how poorly the economy is likely to do in the future.

According to the Congressional Budget Office (CBO), the federal budget changes in the following ways as the economy changes:[4]

- A reduction in real economic growth or an increase in the unemployment rate will lead to a decrease in revenues, an increase in outlays, and an increase in the deficit.

- An increase in inflation will lead to an increase in both revenues and outlays, but the effect on revenues will be greater than on outlays so that, on balance, an increase in inflation will lead to a smaller deficit.

- An increase in interest rates will lead to increases in revenues and outlays. In this case, however, the revenue effect is small, and the overall effect is to increase the deficit.

Economic assumptions have been a source of constant confusion and controversy over the past few years. Since the president, the House and Senate Budget Committees, and CBO generally use different economic projections, their budgets are not always comparable. For example, the Reagan fiscal 1983 budget had a deficit of $91.5 billion that assumed that in 1983 unemployment would be 7.6 percent, inflation would be 5.1 percent, and GNP would grow by 5.2 percent after taking inflation into account. Using its own economic assumptions that differed substantially from the president's, CBO reestimated the deficit to be $120.6 billion or almost $30 billion more. Both of these deficit estimates were for the same budget and included the same proposed spending cuts and increases.

Appendix C provides detailed estimates for the impact on revenues, outlays, and the deficit of four changes in the economy.

Budget Function

The Congressional Budget Act requires both the president's budget and concurrent resolutions on the budget to display all programs according to the principal national need that they are intended to serve. These needs comprise general areas of federal activity (agriculture, defense, health, etc.) and are referred to as "functions." Every program is placed in the one function of the budget that best describes its most important purpose, regardless of the agency or department that administers the program.

A number of misconceptions about budget functions need to be cleared up. First, a function is not the same as the budget of a particular department. The National Defense function, for example, is different from the Department of Defense, because the function also includes some atomic energy programs administered by the Department of Energy. Second, a department's budget usually is part of a number of different functions. The Treasury Department, for instance, administers programs in eight different functions, including Commerce and Housing Credit, General Government, and International Affairs. Finally, a function does not correspond precisely to an authorization or appropriation bill, which usually deals with parts of several different functions at the same time.

Each function is separated into subfunctions, which divide the programs according to the "major mission" they fulfill. The first two digits of a subfunction are the same as the main function; only the last digit is different. For example, function 400: Transportation, contains the following four subfunctions: 401: Ground Transportation; 402: Air Transportation; 403: Water Transportation; and 407: Other Transportation.

Part 5 of the *Budget of the United States Government* describes the budget by function. Part 8 lists all programs according to the department or agency administering them. Appendix D of this book describes each function and includes a list of the major agencies, departments, and programs each contains.

The functions in the budget have both a title and number designation as follows:

Functions of the 1984 Budget

Number	Title
050	National Defense
150	International Affairs
250	General Science, Space, and Technology
270	Energy
300	Natural Resources and Environment
350	Agriculture
370	Commerce and Housing Credit
400	Transportation
450	Community and Regional Development
500	Education, Training, Employment, and Social Services
550	Health
600	Income Security
700	Veterans Benefits and Services
750	Administration of Justice
800	General Government
850	General Purpose Fiscal Assistance
900	Net Interest
920	Allowances
950	Undistributed Offsetting Receipts

PART ONE

THE CONGRESSIONAL BUDGET PROCESS

CHAPTER 2

OVERVIEW

To understand how Congress now considers the budget each year, it is best to review briefly the difficulties that led to the passage of the Congressional Budget and Impoundment Control Act (Public Law 93-344) in 1974. Six main problems had been hampering Congress's consideration of spending and tax legislation.

1. Congress did not have enough time to complete work on all budget bills before the start of the fiscal year. Congress generally convened in January; the president submitted his budget several weeks later; and the fiscal year began on July 1. Congress had only five months, therefore, to do the needed work on spending and tax legislation; and most of these bills were not passed in final form before the start of the fiscal year. This caused continual confusion in the departments and agencies whose budgets were awaiting final consideration.

2. Congress had no ability to set spending priorities. No single committee in either the House or Senate was empowered to review the entire budget, to weigh competing spending demands, or to propose an overall fiscal policy. Instead, Congress debated and voted on each authorization and appropriations bill separately,[1] without any idea of what the other spending proposals might be. The independence of the authorizing committees and appropriations subcommittees enabled each to conduct its business with little regard for the spending intentions of the others. Since each committee and subcommittee viewed its own importance as directly related to the budget increases it achieved for programs under its jurisdiction, committees had even less incentive to work cooperatively.

3. Congress had no ability to set economic policy. Closely related to its inability to establish spending priorities was Congress's inability to determine or adopt an appropriate economic policy. The independence of the authorizing committees and Appropriations Committees was minimal compared to that of the revenue-raising committees (Ways and Means in the House, Finance in the Senate), which generally conducted their work concurrently with the authorization and appropriation process and, therefore, without considering the overall level of spending being proposed. Consequently, fiscal policies could not be planned. The deficit or surplus could not even be projected until all appropriations, all other spending bills, and tax legislation were passed in final form. Because of the short time Congress had to consider these bills, this generally came well after the fiscal year was under way.

4.   *Objective data on budget matters were not available to Congress.* The Office of Management and Budget (OMB) served as the source of detailed information for the president. Congress lacked such a resource, however, and so was at a serious disadvantage when it came to budget matters. Congress had no staff to match OMB's technical expertise, question its spending estimates, or devise budget alternatives. Without adequate information, Congress could do little more than accept the president's assumptions about the economy and the cost and spending rates of individual programs.

5.   *Congress had no way to impose spending discipline on its committees.* For a number of reasons it was difficult for representatives or senators to successfully oppose or change a spending bill. First, there was no way for Congress to judge if a bill was too high because Congress had nothing with which to compare those bills except the president's budget. Few representatives could make such a comparison, furthermore, because the president's budget and congressional spending legislation were in radically different forms and based upon different assumptions about the economy. Second, the committee proposing legislation usually claimed specialized knowledge in its own area of expertise, thus imposing a particularly severe burden on other representatives and senators who wanted to prove that the committee's actions were somehow inappropriate. In addition, amendments by non-committee members often were not looked upon favorably and sometimes were prohibited entirely. Third, astute committees could hide the real cost of a program either through the judicious use of supplemental appropriations[2] later in the year or through other budget gimmicks. Finally, after a spending bill passed in its final form, there was no way for Congress to change it later (if the economy differed from original projections, for example) if the committee with jurisdiction over that bill refused. Consequently, the only means of imposing fiscal restraint was defeating a bill entirely—an extreme action seldom considered, let alone successful.

6. *Congress had no procedures for overcoming presidential impoundments.* The refusal of a president to spend congressionally approved appropriations for technical reasons was a standard practice and was accepted as a proper use of presidential power. Impoundments became increasingly controversial during the Nixon administration, however, because they were used to an unprecedented extent and because they were used by the president to carry out policy preferences different from the ones expressed by Congress in authorization and appropriations bills. Congress found that it had no process for dealing with this situation other than to go to court to force the money to be spent, an alternative most representatives and senators found cumbersome, time-consuming, and unacceptable.

The budget process Congress created in 1974 dealt directly with each of these six problems as follows:

- The start of the fiscal year was changed from July 1 to October 1 to provide three additional months for the passage of all necessary legislation, and a timetable was established to force all participants in the budget process to produce their work on deadlines.

- Budget Committees were created in both the House and Senate to recommend spending priorities and economic policy and to review the activities of all other committees to ensure that their bills complied with congressional budget goals.

- The Congressional Budget Office was created to provide in-house technical expertise and to devise spending, taxing, and economic policy alternatives.

- A "reconciliation" process was established to impose discipline on committees that exceeded desired spending levels.

- A strict procedure was created not simply enabling Congress to review and approve proposed presidential impoundments but requiring it to do so.

The process consists of four major stages.

STAGE ONE: The President's Budget
January 31 to March 15, 1983

The congressional budget process begins with the submission of the president's budget to Congress. The president's budget is only a proposal, albeit a highly significant one. Because of its packaging into five extensive, cohesive documents, the spending and economic policy it embodies, and the media attention it receives, the president's budget proposal is one of the three most important stages of the congressional budget process.

The president's budget proposal is reviewed by all congressional committees over the next six to eight weeks. By March 15, each committee must submit to the Budget Committee in its own house its "views and estimates" on the legislative actions it probably will take on the budget items within its jurisdiction. These reports are not binding commitments or final decisions but merely a guide for the Budget Committees, which are responsible for weighing competing spending requests. The Budget Committees hold their own hearings on the president's budget proposal and receive additional guidance from both the Joint Economic Committee and CBO, which must submit reports during this stage.

STAGE TWO: The First Concurrent Resolution
March 15 to May 15, 1983

The drafting, debate, and passage of the first concurrent resolution on the budget is the second of the three most significant stages of the congressional budget process and is expected to be completed by May 15. The first resolution is the earliest form of the congressional budget. It embodies Congress's spending priorities and economic policy and is compiled by the Budget Committees based on their review of the president's budget proposal; the March 15th reports from the authorizing and revenue committees, and Appropriations Committees; prior-year spending commitments now coming due; prior-year tax changes now taking effect; and Congress's own determination of national needs.

The first resolution also provides budget guidance for all other committees when they consider their spending or tax legislation and for Congress when it reviews those bills. The spending and revenue targets of the first resolution are only tentative, however, and proposed legislation that exceeds them can be considered and passed.

The first resolution does not contain spending ceilings for individual line items in the budget. Instead, the resolution contains recommended levels for five aggregate totals (budget authority, outlays, revenues, public debt, and deficit/surplus) and nineteen functional areas (defense, health, veterans affairs, etc.).[3] The Budget Committees often make certain assumptions about individual programs when they draft the first resolution, but these assumptions are not binding on either the authorizing committees or Appropriations Committees.

In spite of its tentative nature and nonbinding assumptions, it would be wrong to underestimate the first resolution's importance. The first resolution is the foremost expression of Congress's spending priorities and, except in extreme circumstances, those priorities are seldom significantly changed later in the budget process.

As part of the effort to speed up congressional budget activities, the Budget Act requires that all authorization legislation be "reported" (formally proposed) to the House and Senate by May 15, the same date that the first resolution is expected to pass. In addition, neither house is permitted to consider any appropriations bill until the first resolution passes. The reason for this provision is obvious: The first resolution would be useless if appropriations were considered before spending priorities were determined and before the device by which they were measured was put into place.

The first resolution does not require the president's signature to take effect. It is not, therefore, subject to a veto.

STAGE THREE: Authorizations and Appropriations

May 15 to September 12, 1983

Between the passage of the first concurrent resolution and seven days after Labor Day, Congress is expected to complete action on all authorizations and appropriations. Unlike the budget resolutions, these bills include the actual commitments of federal funds to specific programs and, because they require the president's signature to become law, can be vetoed. Regardless of what is assumed in the first concurrent resolution, no program can be implemented unless it is authorized and then money is appropriated for it (see chapter 1). Although the authorizing committees and Appropriations Committees have made several informal accommodations since the congressional budget process began, this part of the process was left substantially the same as before the Budget Act was implemented.

OMB must submit to Congress the midyear review of the president's budget proposal, in the middle of this stage, by July 15. The midyear review includes reestimates of projected spending levels and updated forecasts of the economy. Importantly, however, the midyear review updates the president's budget, not the first budget resolution, and often is little more than a reaffirmation of the original presidential proposal. Because of congressional actions since that time, the midyear review may, therefore, no longer be pertinent.

STAGE FOUR: The Second Concurrent Resolution
September 12 to September 15, 1983

In late summer the Budget Committees hold more hearings primarily to review congressional actions and any changes in the economy since the passage of the first resolution. The Budget Committees then draft the "second concurrent resolution on the budget," which is expected to pass by September 15—fifteen days before the start of the fiscal year on October 1. Unlike the first resolution, the second sets an absolute ceiling on spending and a floor on revenues. Any bill that would cause spending to exceed or revenues to fall below the level established in the second budget resolution is subject to a point of order.[4]

When the Budget Act was passed it was thought that the binding nature of the second resolution, combined with its ability to revise the first resolution, would make this resolution the prime expression of congressional spending priorities and, therefore, the most important part of the budget process. In practice, the drafting of the second resolution has been little more than an accounting exercise. The Budget Committees have simply adjusted the first resolution for any changes in the economy or congressional actions that differed significantly from the assumptions on which it was based.[5] In part this was because of the Budget Committees' initial unwillingness to attempt to use the reconciliation procedures of the Budget Act to directly challenge the other committees. It was easier and politically more prudent for the Budget Committees to accommodate the wishes of these committees than to incur their wrath. The Budget Committees also realized that nothing had changed drastically since the passage of the first resolution less than four months earlier. Consequently, the first resolution has emerged as the principal congressional budget legislation.

Like the first resolution, the second does not require the president's signature and takes effect as soon as it is passed by both houses in its final form. After passage of the second resolution and completion of any reconciliation actions, it is not in order for either the House or Senate to consider legislation that would increase spending above or reduce revenues below the limits set in the resolution. Congress can, however, revise the second resolution to accommodate any such proposals by passing a third (or fourth, fifth, etc.) budget resolution later in the year.

Congress cannot adjourn "sine die" (for the last time at the end of a session) until it has completed all action on the second budget resolution and any reconciliation bills.

Reconciliation

Reconciliation enforces the spending and revenue policies of a budget resolution. As originally envisioned, reconciliation takes place if the second budget resolution establishes spending ceilings below or revenue floors above those that result from the authorization, appropriation, and tax bills passed by Congress since the passage of the first resolution in May. Committees in whose jurisdiction changes are ordered must comply with the instructions of the second resolution. If they refuse, the Budget Committees can in certain circumstances propose necessary spending cuts or tax increases for them.

Reconciliation took on dramatically increased importance in 1981 and 1982 when it was used to enforce the first resolution rather than the second. This was the centerpiece of the Reagan administration's budget strategy in Congress. It enabled the president to achieve virtually all of the spending and tax changes he wanted in a single vote. This tactic greatly increased the importance of the first resolution since reconciliation effectively transformed its targets into binding totals.[6]

Like a budget resolution, reconciliation instructions do not specify individual program changes, although the Budget Committees usually do make assumptions about how the reconciliation will be achieved. These assumptions can be altered or ignored by the committees responsible for the areas of the budget in which the changes are to occur, however, as long as the total reduction (or increase) equals or exceeds the requirements.

Because reconciliation was not envisioned by the framers of the Budget Act to be ordered in the first resolution, no time limit exists for Congress to comply should it occur. Reconciliation actions ordered in the second resolution are expected to be completed by September 25, ten days after the passage of the second resolution and five days before the start of the fiscal year.

Table 3 shows the expected timetable for all congressional actions on the fiscal 1984 budget.

Impoundments

Impoundment procedures included in the Budget Act are not necessarily part of the annual congressional budget process. They are im-

TABLE 3
FISCAL 1984 CONGRESSIONAL BUDGET PROCESS

Deadline	Action
January 31, 1983	President submits his budget to Congress.
March 15	Congressional committees submit their "views and estimates" to the Budget Committees.
April 1	Congressional Budget Office submits its analysis of the president's budget proposal to the Budget Committee.
April 15	Budget Committees report first concurrent budget resolution for fiscal 1983 to their respective houses.
May 15	Congress completes action on first concurrent resolution for fiscal 1983.
July 15	Office of Management and Budget (OMB) submits midyear review of the president's budget proposal.
September 12	Congress completes action on all appropriations bills.
September 15	Congress completes action on second concurrent resolution on the budget for fiscal 1984.
September 25	If needed, Congress completes action on any reconciliation measures.
October 1, 1983	Fiscal 1984 begins.

Note: These are the expected dates. In recent years many steps of the budget process have been seriously delayed.

plemented only when the president proposes either to not spend at all or to delay the spending of funds that previously were approved. In both cases Congress must be notified of the proposal and has the power to force the president to spend the money.

A "rescission" is a presidential proposal not to spend an appropriation that has been provided by Congress. The reason for such a proposal can either be specific (when the objectives of the program can be achieved without spending the full amount appropriated, for example) or general (fiscal policy considerations, for example). Regardless of the reason, the president must submit a message to Congress requesting the rescission and explaining the reasons for the request. If both houses of Congress do not pass a bill approving the proposed rescission within forty-five legislative days, the president must spend the money as originally intended.

A "deferral" is a presidential proposal to delay the spending of congressionally approved appropriations. The delay can be for any length of time but cannot last through the end of the fiscal year. Regardless of the length of time involved, the president must submit a deferral message to Congress. Unlike a rescission, however, which requires specific approval by both houses of Congress, a deferral is automatically assumed to be approved unless, at any time after the president's message has been received, either the House or Senate passes legislation specifically disapproving it.

The Budget and Appropriations Committees in the Senate and the Appropriations Committee in the House have assumed responsibility for reviewing presidential rescission and deferral messages. But the real monitor of this part of the process is the comptroller general, the head of the General Accounting Office (GAO), who

> . . . must review each message and advise the Congress of the facts surrounding the action and its probable effects. In the case of deferrals he must state whether the deferral is, in his view, in accordance with existing statutory authority. The Comptroller General is also required to report to the Congress reserve or deferral action which has not been reported by the president; and to report and reclassify any incorrect transmittals by the president. *Such reports by the Comptroller General have the same legal effect as rescission or deferral messages from the president.*[7] (emphasis added)

The comptroller general also has the power to bring a civil action to force the president to spend the appropriation if he or she refuses to do so after Congress has formally disapproved a proposed rescission or deferral.

The budget process was under a great deal of strain in 1981 and 1982 as Congress and the president battled over the administration's landmark spending and tax proposals and as the economy worsened. The process was used in several different ways, and some of the problems that had plagued Congress's consideration of the budget before 1974 reappeared. The next six chapters discuss all these recent changes and developments in each stage of the budget process.

CHAPTER 3

STAGE ONE: THE PRESIDENT'S BUDGET

Deadline	Action
January 31, 1983	President submits his fiscal 1984 budget proposal to Congress.
March 15	Congressional committees submit their "views and estimates" to the Budget Committees.

The congressional budget process for fiscal 1984 began on January 31, 1983, when President Reagan submitted his proposed budget to Congress. This initial step is quite significant. Despite the fact that the Congressional Budget and Impoundment Control Act of 1974 was passed to limit the president's power on the budget, it did not change the single most important component of his or her spending authority, that is, the power to design a cohesive budget embodying an economic program and spending priorities, and to present it in five budget documents. These documents become the focus of attention on the federal budget.

The budget the president submitted to Congress resulted from months of deliberations and compromises between the White House, OMB, and various agencies and departments. After the president provides initial general guidance, OMB becomes the final arbiter for the vast majority of choices that must be made. This is true both when OMB reviews the proposed internal budgets of each agency and department and when it must decide between competing spending demands of different departments. In a limited number of cases, cabinet members can appeal directly to the president when a highly controversial OMB decision goes against them.

This executive budget process is considerably less open than the congressional budget process and, consequently, difficult to describe precisely. Other than the deadline for submitting the budget to Congress (within fifteen days after it convenes in January), which is set by the Congressional Budget Act, no dates are fixed by law by which time certain decisions have to be made. In addition, the relative importance of decisions made earlier in the executive process varies greatly from agency to agency and program to program, depending on the personalities, political skills, and relative power positions of the decision makers. For example, one agency may have no choice but to accept an OMB decision, while another may be able to get either a further OMB review, or to appeal it to the president.

The budget preparations of the Reagan administration in 1981 are prime examples. In early 1981, OMB and its director, David Stockman, were preeminent forces in compiling the fiscal 1982 budget, in large part because the department secretaries had just been appointed and knew relatively little about the programs they were to administer.[1] Later in 1981, however, Stockman was overruled by the president in favor of Secretary of Defense, Caspar Weinberger, when OMB proposed cuts in defense spending. During the preparations for the 1983 budget in November and December 1981, Stockman was overruled repeatedly when agency and department heads, notably Secretary of Housing and Urban Development, Samuel Pierce, and Environmental Protection Agency Administrator, Ann Gorsuch, also appealed OMB proposed cuts.[2]

The budget that the president submitted to Congress is only a proposal. It will be debated, amended, and even ignored at times by Congress during its deliberations over the next nine months. But virtually all congressional budget activities that take place over the rest of the process will, either formally or informally, use the president's budget as a starting point for debate. More importantly, the large majority of minute decisions made in compiling the president's budget will not be reviewed by Congress because of a lack of interest, staff, and time. Therefore, regardless of what Congress may do to alter the budget at the different stages of its own process, to a very large extent the president will continue to dominate most spending matters.

This certainly was the case with the 1982 budget. Before leaving office, President Carter submitted his budget on January 15, 1981, and Congress could have used it to begin its deliberations. Rather than taking the initiative, Congress waited for the incoming Reagan administration to release the details of its budget proposal on March 10, almost two months after the Carter budget was submitted. This allowed the new president to determine the agenda and seriously delayed the rest of the budget process, making it impossible for Congress to make all the necessary decisions before the start of the fiscal year.[3]

It also was true with the 1983 budget. The initial Reagan proposal was submitted in early February and was immediately criticized and discredited. Instead of proceeding with its own deliberations, however, the House and Senate delayed its budget process until negotiations between key administration and congressional leaders (the so-called "gang of 17") broke up unsuccessfully. It was only in May that congressional deliberations on the budget began in earnest.

Congressional hearings on the budget will further emphasize the president's budget agenda, since the initial witnesses before almost all committees will usually be administration officials. An administration often appears to be conducting the political equivalent of a traveling road show, with key officials (the director of the OMB, the chairman of the Council of Economic Advisers, and the secretary of the Treasury, for example) testifying together or on consecutive days before many different committees. These hearings will take place during the first four weeks after the president's budget is sumitted to Congress.

Congressional hearings on the budget will go in two different directions. The Budget Committees will hold hearings to consider the whole budget. Besides hearing from administration officials, they are likely to receive testimony from outside economists with different views on what the appropriate budget policy should be, interest groups concerned with particular aspects of the budget, other members of Congress, and CBO, which is required by the Budget Act to analyze the president's budget and formally report to Congress.[4] The authorizing committees and Appropriations Committees mostly will hold hearings on the specific parts of the budget within their legislative jurisdiction. They are likely to hear from the cabinet officials whose programs they must review, groups who either benefit from or are otherwise interested in those programs, and other members of Congress.

Before passage of the Congressional Budget Act, all of this activity took place over many months. The Appropriations Committees in particular spent a great deal of time reviewing the budget requests of each department and agency. The benefit of this line-by-line review was that Congress was able to examine the spending plans in detail. But an extraordinary amount of time was necessary to do the work. Appropriations bills usually were not passed in final form before the fiscal year began, and sometimes not until it was well under way.

In part to deal with this problem, the Budget Act requires that all standing committees report to their respective Budget Committees no later than March 15 their "views and estimates" of the actions they probably will take on the provisions of the president's budget within their jurisdictions.[5] Each of these committees must, therefore, complete within eight weeks a large part of the work that previously might have taken six months or more. But because Congress generally is in session only on Tuesday, Wednesday, and Thursday at this point in the year, and because there is a recess scheduled to coincide with the Lincoln and Washington birthday holidays, the amount of time available to review the president's budget actually is considerably less than eight weeks. Obviously, this severely limits the level of detail each committee can consider.

The March 15 reports are not binding commitments by the committees but merely their best estimate as of that date of the actions they might take this session. This includes support for and deviations from presidential recommendations and committee initiatives not included by the president in the budget proposal. The committees are required by the Budget Act to include an estimate of the budget authority and outlays that will be needed for the legislation it expects to pass. Appendix B contains the March 15 reports for fiscal 1983 from the House Armed Services and Foreign Affairs Committees.

The March 15 reports are the first official congressional response to the president's proposals and, therefore, the initial move away from an executive budget. The actual value of the reports varies greatly from committee to committee. Some committees will meet to vote on specific matters to be incorporated in their report and will include detailed backup materials, justifications, and even supplemental and minority views by individual members who either disagree with or wish to distinguish themselves in some other way from the majority position. These committees actually make an attempt to determine spending priorities and provide real guidance to their Budget Committees. Other committees make no such attempt in the belief that any decisions would be premature and might limit their options in the future. This type of report is, of course, of minimal value and often indicates that the committee feels dissatisfied with the budget process or Budget Committee.

Nevertheless the March 15 reports are an often overlooked and undervalued part of the budget process. They force the authorizing committees and Appropriations Committees to review and quickly make some initial decisions about the president's budget. They provide the Budget Committees with guidance as to the intentions of the committees. And, because of the limited time the committees have to review the president's budget and make their report to the Budget Committee, the March 15 reports often identify those issues within each committee's purview that, because they specifically have been raised, are likely to be controversial or, because they have been ignored entirely or glossed over, are likely not to be considered at all.

Again, it is important to remember that these reports are not binding in any way on the committees that make them. Issues that may be unimportant in March may well be highly controversial later in the year when the actual authorizations and appropriations are being debated. Or the House committee may view an item as being worthy of further discussion, and its Senate counterpart may not.

The March 15 reports acquire additional importance because the Budget Act requires that authorizations not previously enacted be considered and voted on by the authorizing committees and formally proposed or "reported" to their respective houses by May 15. This provision will be discussed in the next chapter. However, it is important to mention it here as well because it limits the time an authorizing committee has after submitting its March 15 report to review its decisions. As in the period leading up to the March 15 deadline, a recess (for Easter/Passover) and Congress's continued three-day Washington work schedule make this two-month period from March 15 to May 15 even shorter. The result is to make the March 15 report and each committee's deliberations leading to it a highly significant part of the overall congressional budget process.

For the same reason that much of the president's budget will not be debated by Congress, a good deal of the detail necessary to compile the March 15 reports also will not be reviewed further either by the individual committees or by the House, Senate, or full Congress. There simply is not enough time to reconsider questions on which no substantial controversy has arisen or that are insignificant when compared to the larger budget issues that must be debated.

This means that the earlier a particular item or program can be included in the budget, the better are its chances of staying there. If, for example, a new office in the Department of Defense is included in the presidential budget proposal and is specifically included in the March 15 reports, the likelihood of its ultimately being funded is increased significantly. On the other hand, an attempt to add that same office in the authorization or appropriation bill after it was not included in the president's budget or was specifically rejected from the March 15 report will make the job much more difficult. Therefore, in spite of the fact that the president's budget submission is only a proposal, and that the March 15 reports are nonbinding, significant budget decisions are made at both of these points in the process.

The March 15 reports are submitted by the committees to their respective Budget Committees, which do not hold separate hearings on the reports but compile them into a single volume and make them available to other members of Congress and to the public. These reports receive only minimal attention by the media, in no way approaching the notice received by the president's budget. The reports then become one of several considerations used by the Budget Committees to compile the first concurrent resolution on the budget, as described in the next chapter.

CHAPTER 4

STAGE TWO: THE FIRST CONCURRENT RESOLUTION ON THE BUDGET

Deadline	Action
April 15	Budget Committees report first concurrent resolution on the budget for fiscal 1984 to their respective houses.
May 15	Congress completes action on the first concurrent resolution on the budget for fiscal 1984.
May 15	Committees report authorization bills to their respective houses.

The first concurrent resolution on the budget does not actually appropriate money or firmly determine spending priorities. Its aggregate and functional totals are not binding on congressional actions. It is supposed to be revised in less than four months by the second concurrent resolution. However, the first budget resolution has become the single most important budget decision Congress makes each year, and the foremost expression of congressional spending priorities.

The first concurrent resolution on the budget, which is expected to pass by May 15, is the congressional budget in its earliest form. According to section 301(a) of the Budget Act, the first resolution for any fiscal year must specify:[1]

1. The appropriate level of budget authority and outlays for the total budget;

2. An estimate of the level of budget authority and outlays for each functional category of the budget;[2]

29

3. The recommended level of revenues;

4. The surplus or deficit; and

5. The appropriate level of the public debt.

It is important to emphasize that none of these figures is final. They are only *tentative* decisions on fiscal policy matters that will be used by Congress to determine whether a proposed authorization, appropriations, or revenue bill is in keeping with the priorities it establishes. Legislation proposed later in the year that exceeds the aggregate and functional totals of the first resolution can, therefore, be considered and passed.

This critical feature of the first resolution can be best understood by recalling the circumstances surrounding the consideration and passage of the Budget Act. It was politically impossible to give the Budget Committees the authority to impose a budget on the authorizing and tax committees, and on the Appropriations Committees, before they had an opportunity to pass their legislation, since that would have made these actions superfluous. On the other hand, a budget that was passed after the authorization, appropriations, and tax bills were final would have made it meaningless. The solution was first to pass a nonbinding budget that would be used to guide the committees in their work but that would not restrict them in any formal way, and then, after the bills were in final form, to pass another, binding budget. That, in theory, is the purpose of the first concurrent resolution: It is a preliminary spending plan; a target for the authorizing and tax committees, and Appropriations Committees, to aim at when they compile their bills; and a measuring device for Congress to judge how well those committees have followed its tentatively expressed spending priorities.

In practice, however, the consideration and passage of the first resolution has become a much more significant step in the budget process. As is explained in chapter 6, it was the second resolution that was expected to be the more important expression of congressional budget policy since its figures were a firm spending ceiling and a revenue floor, and any legislation violating them was subject to a point of order. As the budget process has been implemented, however, the second resolution generally has become nothing more than an updated version of the first. Its drafting has been little more than pro forma, with the first resolution simply being adjusted for any changes in the economy and congressional actions that deviated from the assumptions on which it was based. The major congressional budget decisions on both the aggregates and functions are, therefore, really made in the first resolution. Congress seldom changes them substantially.

Even the extreme circumstances of fiscal 1982 did not induce Congress to change the first resolution when it drafted the second. The first resolution for fiscal 1982 contained a $37.7 billion deficit, as the Reagan administration had projected. But before the second resolution could be considered, most analysts were projecting a deficit of over $100 billion. In spite of this 270 percent increase, Congress decided not to make any changes in the first resolution's estimates when it passed the second resolution.

For fiscal 1983 the situation was even worse. Recognizing the likely difficulty in passing a second budget resolution only two months before the 1982 elections, Congress included a provision in the first resolution that automatically made it the second resolution for that year when Congress failed to pass a new second resolution by October 1. Congress never even tried to pass a second resolution, although the deficit had ballooned from the first resolution's estimate of $103.9 billion to approximately $155 billion.

The first resolution is compiled by the Budget Committees after they review a number of sources of information, in particular the president's budget proposal and the March 15 reports from the different committees. They also consider the testimony from their own hearings, any changes in the economy since the president's budget was submitted to them, public support for or against presidential initiatives, spending reestimates of the president's budget and other information provided by CBO, and the wishes of their own members. Many of the Budget Committees' deliberations, however, are based on information they receive informally from colleagues on other committees about their wants, needs, and intentions on budget-related matters. The Budget Committees' chairpersons will meet with the chairpersons of the other committees, and Budget Committee staff members will talk with their counterparts about likely spending actions.[3] This is necessary because the Budget Committees cannot simply propose a budget, as the president did in January. Instead they must report a spending plan that will be acceptable to a majority of the House and Senate.

To facilitate this acceptance, and to avoid the appearance that the Budget Committees are usurping the substantive jurisdiction of the other committees, the first resolution makes decisions only on the aggregate and functional totals; *it makes no line-by-line or program decisions.* The Budget Committees may make certain assumptions about a particular program as the resolution is drafted, but those assumptions are not in any way binding.

This will not appear to be the case for anyone watching the Budget Committees debate and draft ("mark up") the first resolution. Amendments will be offered and much of the discussion will center on individual programs and even parts of programs. All of these amendments and discussions, however, are based only on an assumption that the relevant committee ultimately will do what the Budget Committee expects. But it is only the aggregate and functional totals of the first budget resolution that actually are affected by an amendment. This is true even if the Budget Committee specifies its assumptions in committee, in the report accompanying the first resolution, during debate on the floor of the House or Senate, or in the conference report. The authorizing committees and Appropriations Committees are free to follow the assumptions if they wish, or to ignore them entirely, as long as they stay within the overall totals allocated to them.

The House and Senate Budget Committees have approached the job of marking up the first budget resolution very differently. In the House, the chairman of the committee has compiled a "chairman's mark," a lengthy document that contains recommendations for the budget authority and outlays for each function and for the budget as a whole. A typical functional recommendation from the chairman's mark shows the amount recommended in the president's budget; the CBO "current policy" baseline;[4] the issues on which the chairman disagrees with the president, including the differences in budget authority and outlays; and the net total for the function after the budget implications of all these issues are added together. It is this total that is the starting point for the debate on each function, and members can offer amendments to it if they disagree with the chairman.

Table 4 is from the fiscal 1983 chairman's mark used by the House Budget Committee when it reviewed function 400: Transportation and is typical of what it uses each year. First, a multiyear perspective is included that depicts the actual level of spending for the past four years, estimates for the current year, and the proposed level for the upcoming year with the implications of that proposal for the following two years.[5] The information clearly shows the differences between the baseline, the president's recommendation, and the chairman's mark.

Next, table 4 shows how the chairman derived his mark. It includes the CBO baseline as revised by House Budget Committee analysts, the major issues the chairman decided to address, and the chairman's final recommendation.

Finally, table 4 shows a relatively new feature of the chairman's mark—the credit programs of the function. The table shows individual programs and summarizes them according to the concepts of the credit budget.[6] In both instances the chairman's mark is compared to the CBO baseline and the president's recommendation.

TABLE 4
FUNCTION 400: TRANSPORTATION

II. MULTIYEAR PERSPECTIVE

In billions of dollars	Budget Authority	Outlays
Fiscal Year 1978 Actual....................	15.05	15.45
Fiscal Year 1979 Actual....................	19.20	17.45
Fiscal Year 1980 Actual....................	20.20	21.10
Fiscal Year 1981 Actual....................	24.90	23.40
Fiscal Year 1982 Second Budget Resolution (12/9/81).	21.20	20.40
Fiscal Year 1982 President's Request (4/9/82)......	20.90	21.15
Fiscal Year 1982 Chairman's Recommendation......	21.35	21.45
Fiscal Year 1983:		
President's Request (4/9/82).............	18.95	19.55
CBO Baseline......................	22.30	20.45
Chairman's Recommendation.............	21.95	20.00
Fiscal Year 1984:		
President's Plan (4/9/82)..............	18.95	18.60
CBO Baseline......................	23.30	21.20
Chairman's Recommendation.............	22.05	19.65
Fiscal Year 1985:		
President's Plan (4/9/82)..............	19.25	19.20
CBO Baseline......................	24.35	22.40
Chairman's Recommendation.............	22.60	19.85

TABLE 4 (continued)

III. Summary of Recommendation

In billions of dollars	FY 1983 Budget		FY 1984 Plan		FY 1985 Plan	
	BA	O	BA	O	BA	O
Current Policy Baseline..............	22.30	20.45	23.30	21.20	24.35	22.40
Adjustments⟋............	+0.55	+0.25	+0.60	+0.40	+0.65	+0.50
Revised Baseline.............	22.85	20.70	23.90	21.60	25.00	22.90

Major Policy Issues

1. Effect of Discretionary Program Freeze............ | -0.70 | -0.50 | -1.35 | -1.45 | -1.90 | -2.55

The savings indicate the effect of maintaining discretionary programs in this function at the fiscal year 1982 program level for the next three years. The recommendation assumes that within the overall totals, funding levels for individual programs will be determined through the annual appropriations process.

For illustrative purposes, a table following this summary displays the effect of the freeze if applied uniformly to major programs within this function.

TABLE 4 (continued)

2. Other Policy Issues..............	-0.20	-0.20	-0.50	-0.50	-0.50	-0.50
• Coast Guard User Fees............	(-0.20)	(-0.20)	(-0.50)	(-0.50)	(-0.50)	(-0.50)
This proposal assumes first time enactment of a Coast Guard Boat and Yacht user fee proposed in the President's budget. The proposal would be phased in, beginning in fiscal year 1983.						
Subtotal, Changes from Current Policy Baseline...............	(-0.90)	(-0.70)	(-1.85)	(-1.95)	(-2.40)	(-3.05)
CHAIRMAN'S RECOMMENDATION..............	21.95	20.00	22.05	19.65	22.60	19.85

1/ Adjustments for impact of 1982 supplementals not included in CBO baseline.

TABLE 4 (continued)

1983 Credit Budget Recommendation

(In millions of dollars)

Program	Gross Direct Loan Obligations			Gross Loan Guarantee Commitments		
	CBO Baseline	President's April Budget	HBC Recom.	CBO Baseline	President's April Budget	HBC Recom.
Rail Rehabilitation and Improvement.........	114	...	106	293	...	135
Aircraft Purchase Loans...	...	...	...	120	...	111
Federal Ship Financing Fund.............	25	25	25	740	600	675
Federal Financing Bank....	280	58	173	...	...	...
All Other...............	95	34	58	3	...	...
TOTAL.................	514	117	362	1,156	600	921

SUMMARY OF RECOMMENDATION
(In billions of dollars)

Loan Guarantee Commitments:	CBO Baseline	President's April Budget	HBC Recom.
Gross Guarantee Commitments	1.15	0.60	0.90
Less Secondary Guarantees	-*	...	...
Less Guarantees of Direct Loans	-0.25	-0.05	-0.15
Primary Loan Guarantee Commitments	0.90	0.55	0.75

Direct Loan Obligations:	CBO Baseline	President's April Budget	HBC Recom.
On-budget	0.20	0.05	0.20
Off-budget	0.30	0.05	0.15
Subtotal, gross direct loans	0.50	0.10	0.35
Less Loan Assets sold to FFB	...	...	...
Net Direct Loans	0.50	0.10	0.35

*Less than $25 million

Reprinted from U.S. House of Representatives, Committee on the Budget, "Chairman's Recommendations for the First Concurrent Resolution on the Fiscal Year 1983 Budget and a Fiscal Year 1984 and Fiscal Year 1985 Budget Plan and a Revised Second Concurrent Resolution for Fiscal Year 1982," May 12, 1982, pp. 103–105.

Using these materials the House Budget Committee reviews all of the functions twice. Any preliminary decisions made in the first round can be redebated in the second, at which point the final vote approving the function is taken. No vote on the five aggregates (budget authority, outlays, revenues, surplus/deficit, and level of public debt) is taken until the functions are decided, although a chart is displayed throughout the markup proceedings showing these figures. The amounts to be spent on each function are not, therefore, tailored to fit within totals that first are determined to be appropriate for the assumed economic conditions. Instead, the totals are derived from the sum of the nineteen different functions and then voted on by the committee.

The Senate Budget Committee's markup process is considerably less detail-oriented than the one used by the House Budget Committee. The materials change from year to year depending on the presentation that the committee believes is easiest for the members to understand and most suitable for the situation. In general the materials adjust the current year budget in different ways *without making a specific recommendation.* Usually they

> ... distinguish between adjustments mandated by law (current law estimates) and the additional cost of adjusting all programs for inflation (current policy). Moreover, the documents . . . show the spending adjustments attributable to changes in workload. With these modifications, [the Senate Budget Committee] has alternative baselines for marking up its resolutions. It can use the higher current policy numbers or the lower current law levels. It can provide only for workload increases or it can add funds to account for inflation or to improve programs.[7]

Table 5 is from the fiscal 1983 markup book used by the Senate Budget Committee when it reviewed function 400: Transportation. The differences between it and the House Budget Committee's information for the same function are striking. There is no single recommendation, just a series of options that include the baseline, the president's proposal, and nine other proposals from members of the committee. The specific assumptions about what is included in or excluded from each proposal is not immediately apparent.[8] It is the baseline that generally is used as the starting point for the committee's deliberations, and the members are free to recommend changes in it based on any of the listed plans, or on any other proposal.

Like the House Budget Committee, the Senate Budget Committee markup also goes through multiple rounds, but much of the debate in the later rounds focuses on the budget aggregates that result from the initial decisions on the different functions. Functions are reopened as senators feel the need to change the totals in some way.

TABLE 5
FUNCTION 400: TRANSPORTATION
Summary of Budget Options
($ billions)

| | FY 1982 | |
	BA	O
Revised baseline.....................	20.8	21.3

Total budget plans

Revised baseline adjusted to exclude discretionary inflation...........	20.8	21.3
Change from revised baseline..	---	---
President's request re-estimated by CBO............................	20.8	21.3
Change from revised baseline..	-(*)	+(*)
Senator Domenici...................	20.8	21.3
Change from revised baseline..	---	---
Senator Hollings...................	20.8	21.3
Change from revised baseline..	---	---
Senator Boschwitz...................	20.8	21.3
Change from revised baseline..	---	---

TABLE 5 (continued)

FY 1983		FY 1984		FY 1985	
BA	O	BA	O	BA	O
22.3	20.5	23.3	21.2	24.3	22.4

21.3	19.9	21.6	19.6	22.1	19.7
-1.0	-0.6	-1.7	-1.6	-2.3	-2.7
19.1	19.4	19.0	18.8	19.2	19.4
-3.2	-1.1	-4.3	-2.4	-5.1	-3.0
21.1	19.7	20.8	18.8	21.2	18.9
-1.2	-0.8	-2.5	-2.4	-3.1	-3.5
22.3	20.5	23.3	21.2	24.3	22.4
-(*)	-(*)	-(*)	-(*)	-(*)	-(*)
21.1	19.7	20.8	18.8	21.2	18.9
-1.2	-0.8	-2.5	-2.4	-3.1	-3.5

TABLE 5 (continued)
FUNCTION 400: TRANSPORTATION
SUMMARY OF BUDGET OPTIONS
($ billions)

	FY 1982	
	BA	O
Total budget plans (continued)		
Senator Kasten....................	20.8	21.3
Change from revised baseline..	---	---
Senator Gorton....................	20.8	21.3
Change from revised baseline..	---	---
Senator Grassley...................	20.8	21.3
Change from revised baseline..	-..-	---
Partial budget plans		
Senate Commerce Committee:		
Specified changes from revised baseline....................	---	---
Senate Environment and Public Works Committee:		
Specified changes from revised baseline....................		
Senator Symms:		
Specified changes from revised baseline....................	---	---

TABLE 5 (continued)

FY 1983		FY 1984		FY 1985	
BA	O	BA	O	BA	O
20.6	19.4	20.5	18.8	21.2	19.4
-1.7	-1.1	-2.8	-2.4	-3.1	-3.0
21.3	19.9	21.6	19.6	22.1	19.7
-1.0	-0.6	-1.7	-1.6	-2.3	-2.7
21.3	19.9	21.6	19.6	22.0	19.6
-1.0	-0.6	-1.7	-1.6	-2.4	-2.8
+0.1	-0.2	+1.3	+0.3	+1.2	+1.0
-0.8	-0.1				
-(*)	-(*)	-(*)	-(*)	-0.1	-0.1

Reprinted from U. S. Senate, Committee on the Budget, "First Budget Resolution for Fiscal Year 1983 Markup Materials," May 3, 1982, pp. 400–1, 400–2, and 400–3.

The budget resolution markups are important not just because of the aggregate and functional totals approved by the Budget Committees but also because of the individual program issues that are debated to reach those totals. Significant momentum often is given to a proposal if the Budget Committee specifically mentions it in its materials and then debates and approves it during the markup. This is true even though the Budget Committees' approval neither authorizes the program nor approves money for it, and the authorizing committees and Appropriations Committees are free to ignore the first resolution's assumptions. However, if they approve the proposal, the Budget Committees will be seen as having "provided room" in the budget for it and showing congressional support.

Of course, the opposite is true for a proposal that specifically is rejected in the markups: There will be less chance of Congress ultimately approving it even though the Budget Committees' assumptions are not binding.

The Budget Act contains very specific rules for floor consideration of the first resolution. In the House, debate can begin no earlier than ten days after the resolution has been reported by the Budget Committee. No more than ten hours of general debate are allowed initially, after which amendments to the resolution may be proposed and are considered under the "five-minute" rule (each member can speak about that amendment for only five minutes). A proposed amendment must be "mathematically consistent," that is, all aggregate and functional totals it seeks to modify must be specified and added to or subtracted from properly.[9]

In each of the past few years the House has adopted several additional rules that have been designed to expedite the floor debate. The most stringent of these rules has limited the amendments that could be offered by requiring them first to be approved by the Rules Committee. Amendments also have been limited by a rule that prohibits amending a function that already has been amended unless the new amendment is "broader" in some way.[10]

In the Senate there is no specified lay-over period between the time the Budget Committee reports the first concurrent resolution and its consideration. A maximum of fifty hours of debate is allowed, with debate on any one amendment limited to two hours. Debate on an amendment to an amendment is limited to only one hour. Mathematical consistency also is required.

If the House and Senate conferees on the first resolution cannot reach complete agreement within seven days, the Budget Act specifies that they report back to their respective houses recommending all matters on which they do agree and reporting those on which they do not.

In practice, however, the seven-day limit has been ignored. The conference report can be debated by the Senate only after a three-day layover, and debate is limited to ten hours. The House also has a three-day layover, but debate is limited to five hours.

Besides the conference report itself, the conferees must also file an accompanying report known as the "Joint Statement of Managers," which, along with explaining the conference report, divides the total budget authority and outlays of the first resolution among the different spending committees in each house. For example, if the conference report provided $10 billion in budget authority and outlays for a function, the joint statement of managers must divide that amount between the different committees with legislative jurisdiction over the programs that make up that function. Each of these committees then must reallocate this amount among its own subcommittees and report this internal allocation back to its respective house. It is these "section 302(A)" allocations[11] that Congress uses to measure how close to the first resolution the different authorization and appropriation bills actually are when they are debated during the year, as described in the next chapter.

CHAPTER 5

STAGE THREE: AUTHORIZATIONS AND APPROPRIATIONS

Deadline	Action
May 15	Committees report authorization bills to their respective houses.
July 15	President submits midyear review of the budget to Congress.
September 12	Congress completes action on all bills providing new budget authority and new spending authority.

The passage of the different authorization and appropriations[1] bills is the first part of the congressional budget process that actually commits the federal government to conducting certain activities and spending money. Until this stage the decisions are tentative and no funds actually are made available: The president's budget is only a proposal, the March 15 reports do not bind the committees that submit them, and the first concurrent resolution is only a target. The authorization-appropriations stage is different, however, since these decisions ordinarily are final and definite.

The Budget Act did not formally change the authorization-appropriations process, for no substantive jurisdiction was taken away from these committees. Instead, the budget process was imposed over them, and a framework was created within which they had to conduct their activities. There are, however, three ways in which the authorization-appropriations stage has been affected—one procedural, one political, and one substantive.

Procedurally, the authorizing committees and Appropriations Committees now have far less time to do their work, since their activities are expected to be completed within fifteen weeks from the time the first resolution is passed in May. This is work that previously might have taken fifteen *months* or longer to complete.

This severe time limit was one way the Budget Act attempted to deal with the problem of not having all authorizations and appropriations in place before the start of the fiscal year (see chapter 2). This provision has not been completely effective, however, partly because the time limitations are too extreme and do not account for the standard congressional recesses for August and Labor Day. Although the act provides a seemingly ample three and one-half months for this stage, in reality the authorizing committees and Appropriations Committees have only ten working weeks.

In addition, Congress often has been debating highly controversial issues that have held up the final passage of one or more appropriations bills, or, because of a delay in passing the first resolution, Congress has been unable to begin this stage promptly on May 15.

In 1982, for example, Congress did not pass the first resolution until mid-June. In 1981 Congress waited until mid-March, when the incoming Reagan administration submitted its changes to the proposed Carter budget, before beginning the budget debate. In 1980 Congress waited until after the November elections before voting on most budget and appropriations matters.

The overall result of these delays has been fewer appropriations bills in place as the fiscal year begins and an increasing reliance on "continuing resolutions," legislation that allows a federal agency or department to continue spending funds when its regular appropriation is not passed on time.[2] Delayed appropriations are one of the problems the budget process was created to avoid, and their renewed occurrence must be considered one of its major failings.

Politically, the budget process places unofficial and nonbinding, yet significant limitations on the authorizing committees. Before passage of the Budget Act, authorization bills were the first step in the congressional spending process. Since there was nothing to compare these bills to except the president's budget proposal, which was in a different form, the authorizing committees were relatively unconstrained. Now, however, the first resolution permits an easy comparison to be made and the suitability of an authorization to be determined. The authorizing committees, therefore, often must explain and justify any proposed deviations from the spending plan passed earlier by Congress. In fact, they often must fight with the Budget Committees, which

have taken it upon themselves to enforce or at least remind their respective houses about the first resolution's targets.

This enforcement role is not mentioned specifically in the Budget
Act, yet it has become an important function of the Budget Committees.
Both committees attempt to accomplish it through behind-the-scenes
activities, with negotiations often conducted before a particular bill
reaches the floor for debate. When these discussions are not successful,
the Budget Committees often try to inform their houses about the budget
implications of the authorizations they are considering. This is precisely the type of debate that could not have taken place before the
budget process was implemented and is a clear indication of its increasing importance to all other congressional activities.

The Budget Committees also monitor appropriations bills, the legislation that actually spends money. Here too their involvement is largely
behind-the-scenes, with most problems negotiated successfully before
a bill reaches the floor for debate. To assist the Budget Committees in
these "scorekeeping" activities, CBO issues periodic reports on how
the appropriations and tax bills, which either have already passed or
are waiting to be considered, compare with the first resolution's targets,
and on any changes in the economy since the resolution passed in May.

The House Budget Committee also issues its own scorekeeping
reports on all appropriations bills. These "Early Warning Reports" are
not distributed widely but often are available to the public upon request.
Their basic purpose is to compare each appropriation with the first
budget resolution so that the members of the committee can determine
whether the bill is in keeping with the already approved fiscal policy.

Substantively, the Budget Act requires the authorizing committees
and Appropriations Committees to include specific budget information
in the reports accompanying their bills. The report for any authorization
bill providing spending authority, all appropriations bills, and any legislation providing new or increased tax expenditures[3] must contain an
estimate of how those bills compare with the first resolution just passed
by Congress. To accomplish this the committees must use the section
302 allocations derived from the conference report on the first resolution (see chapter 4). The reports also must contain estimates of the
spending or tax loss that will occur over the next five years if Congress
passes the bill in its current form. All of these estimates generally are
prepared with CBO's assistance.

As discussed in chapter 3, all of the committees also must submit
reports to their respective Budget Committee as to the actions they
probably will take on the parts of the budget within their jurisdiction.
As the Budget Committees have requested more and more information

in these reports they have become a significant (and sometimes controversial) burden on the authorizing committees and Appropriations Committees, which have been forced to make many decisions in a comparatively short period of time.[4]

The major impact of this part of the budget process has been to make the authorization-appropriations stage more visible. The committees must do their work within a specified period, in such a way that Congress can easily understand and judge how well it complies with previously expressed spending priorities. The Budget Act did not prohibit bills that violate the first resolution from being considered, and authorization and appropriations bills that deviate from it can be debated and passed. The act, however, in effect, requires that these deviations be known and justified in debate, and representatives and senators must go on record as for or against them.

The authorization-appropriations stage also is important because it allows the president again to have a direct influence on the spending decisions made by Congress. The first resolution does not require the president's signature, and the March 15 reports are internal congressional documents. Authorization and appropriations bills, on the other hand, are subject to a veto and thus usually require the first official presidential response to congressional spending priorities.

The president also is required to prepare a budget report during this stage. The "Midyear Review of the Budget," which must be submitted by July 15, is an updated version of the president's budget proposal that incorporates revisions in the administration's original program, changes in the economy, and the final spending and revenue totals for the previous year's budget. The midyear review usually is not considered an important report, however, since it generally does not include congressional changes in the president's budget in its estimates, even if those changes have been passed or if congressional action on an administration proposal is totally unlikely. As a result, the midyear review is seen more as a partisan reaffirmation of the president's program with updated figures rather than as a useful tool for congressional decision making. It receives little attention in Congress or the news media.

As noted, the authorization-appropriations stage is expected to be completed no later than seven days after Labor Day. Then Congress begins consideration of the second concurrent resolution on the budget, as described in the next chapter.

CHAPTER 6

STAGE FOUR: THE SECOND CONCURRENT RESOLUTION ON THE BUDGET

Deadline	Action
September 15	Congress completes action on the second concurrent resolution on the budget.

The second concurrent resolution on the budget was supposed to be the most important step in the budget process. After all the spending bills were passed, it was expected that Congress would make a final decision on the appropriate fiscal policy for the upcoming fiscal year based on any changes in the economy or in spending priorities. To do so, Congress would pass a second budget resolution that was binding on all committees. Any bill that would cause spending to exceed the ceiling or revenues to fall below the floor set by that resolution would be subject to a point of order and would not be considered.

In practice, however, the second resolution has not been as important as expected. Instead of debating and reviewing the budget in its entirety, Congress generally has done little more than revise the first resolution to take into account any changes in spending and revenues that differ from the assumptions on which the resolution was based. Congress has not bothered to make even these minimal changes in recent years. As noted in chapter 4, in 1981 Congress passed a second resolution for fiscal 1982 that simply used the same aggregate and functional totals of the first resolution for that year even though almost no one believed they were still correct. In 1982 Congress did not pass a second resolution at all. Instead, it included a provision in the fiscal

49

1983 first resolution that automatically made it the second resolution for that year when Congress failed to pass a separate second resolution by October 1, 1982.[1]

Because of these changes the second resolution effectively has become nonbinding and has lost virtually all of its significance. Congress has either passed a resolution that simply accommodated all likely spending and taxing actions for the next fiscal year, or it passed a resolution with limits so unrealistic that it was ignored or "waived"[2] when bills were considered.

Even when that is not the case—when economic or political exigencies require different federal budget policies—Congress is not completely bound by the second resolution, since it can pass a third (or fourth, fifth, etc.) budget resolution to revise the previous ceiling and floor. Contrary to the initial expectations, therefore, the second resolution is not the most important of all congressional budget votes.

This downgrading of the second resolution is the result of three factors: the unwillingness of the Budget Committees to test their power and prestige in the early years of the budget process by attempting reconciliation (see chapter 7); the recognized difficulty of implementing the reconciliation procedures of the Budget Act after the appropriations and authorization bills have passed; and, in recent years, the political problem of passing a second budget resolution with a huge increase in the deficit from the first resolution. The result is a second resolution that means little and a first resolution that has grown significantly in importance.

When Congress decides to pass a second resolution the Budget Committees begin their work close to Labor Day when they hold a new round of hearings. These hearings usually do not reexamine individual budget issues that were decided in May. Instead, they focus on the accuracy of the assumptions on which the first resolution was based (especially the likely performance of the economy), congressional actions on the different appropriations bills, and revised rates of spending for particular programs ("spendout rates").

Unlike the procedures it imposes for consideration of the first resolution, the Budget Act does not require each authorizing committee and Appropriations Committee to submit a formal statement to its respective Budget Committee analogous to the March 15 report. Since all appropriations are expected to be passed in final form when the second resolution markup begins, the bills themselves will contain the information needed by the Budget Committees. When an appropriation is not passed by this deadline, the Budget Committees rely on informal communications between their members and staff and the other committees to determine what the likely outcome will be. In some cases the chairperson of the relevant appropriations subcommittee also will send a letter to the Budget Committee outlining his or her views more formally, particularly when the bill differs from a first resolution assumption.

Although Congress drafts the second resolution using this accommodating rather than adversarial process, the votes that determine it are neither automatic nor noncontroversial. Each decision, whether in committee or on the floor, is debated at length, and roll call votes often put the representatives and senators on record as for or against specific budget items and overall totals. Before implementation of the budget process, most of these spending increases would have taken place with members claiming they did not understand the budget implications of their votes. Because of the multiple decisions and votes that now are required before the budget is final (March 15 reports, first resolution, authorization-appropriations, second resolution), this claim no longer is possible.

Both Budget Committees use the same markup procedures for the second resolution as for the first. The House committee works from a chairman's mark, reviews each function twice, and then approves the aggregates. Instead of a chairman's mark, the Senate committee works from various possible starting points (current policy, current law, etc.) and goes through the functions less formally until some consensus is reached (see chapter 4). The procedures for debate by the full House and Senate also are the same as those for the first resolution.

As noted earlier, Congress can pass a resolution to revise the second resolution at any time. The procedures for marking up these additional resolutions are not specified in the Budget Act and have varied from year to year. In general, the Budget Committees have focused only on those functions they wished to change. This does not, however, prohibit representatives and senators from offering amendments to other sections. The procedures for floor debate are the same for these budget resolutions as for the first.

The second resolution is expected to pass in final form by September 15. As is explained in the next chapter, if reconciliation instructions are included in the resolution, the reconciliation bill is expected to pass by September 25, five days before the start of the fiscal year on October 1. Congress cannot adjourn for the last time at the end of the term ("sine die") until it has completed action on the second resolution and any required reconciliation bills.

CHAPTER 7

RECONCILIATION

Deadline	Action
September 25	Congress completes action on reconciliation bill or resolution, if any.

Reconciliation is the controversial process that enables Congress to enforce the spending and tax priorities and totals of a budget resolution. It can best be understood by reviewing two of the difficulties Congress faced before the Budget Act was passed.

First, Congress had no ability to establish a fiscal policy. Second, even if a spending and taxing policy could have been set, Congress had no way of forcing its committees to comply with it (see chapter 2). The spending policy problem was dealt with by requiring the two budget resolutions to be passed. If, however, there was no enforcement procedure, these resolutions (and the budget process) would have been meaningless because the committees could have ignored them.

Reconciliation was designed to make sure this did not happen. It was intended to be used when the second concurrent resolution cut total spending below and/or increased revenues above the levels projected to result from current law.[1] In that case reconciliation language in the second resolution would direct one or more committees to report new legislation that would either cut spending from existing programs or increase revenues as needed. All this work would begin after the second resolution passed on September 15 and be completed no later than September 25, five days before the start of the fiscal year on October 1.

In the early years of the budget process, reconciliation was hardly discussed, let alone attempted, even though the second resolution's ceilings almost always were above the first resolution's targets. This was partly because of the Budget Committees' unwillingness to risk the future of the budget process by antagonizing the authorizing and revenue committees, and the Appropriations Committees which already were suspicious of apparent intrusions into their legislative jurisdictions. The Budget Committees felt that an early defeat of an attempted reconciliation might have the same effect as not including these procedures in the Budget Act at all: The committees would feel free to ignore the fiscal policy of a budget resolution.

A second, related reason was the realization by the Budget Committees that it would be very difficult to achieve reconciliation after the second resolution because (1) the authorization, appropriations, and tax bills for that year already would have passed, and (2) the ten days allowed in the Budget Act to do this work would have been insufficient. This realization was partly responsible for the Budget Committees' decisions to try to enforce the first resolution's targets during the authorization, and appropriations and tax debates, even though these totals were not binding (see chapter 5).

It is understandable, therefore, that in practice, reconciliation has only been used to enforce the targets of the first resolution rather than the ceilings and floors of the second. In the first resolution for fiscal 1981, for example, Congress directed its committees to recommend legislative changes that decreased spending by $5.0 billion in budget authority and $6.5 billion in outlays, and increased revenues by $4.2 billion. In the first concurrent resolution for fiscal 1982, Congress directed its committees to recommend changes in authorizations that resulted in savings of $51.7 billion in budget authority and $35.1 billion in outlays. In the first resolution for fiscal 1983, Congress directed its committees to recommend spending savings of $10.9 billion in budget authority and $27.2 billion in outlays and revenue increases of $98.3 billion over the three-year period of fiscal 1983–1985.[2]

As discussed in chapter 4, the use of reconciliation in the first resolution both further emphasizes that resolution's significance as the foremost expression of congressional budget priorities, and downgrades the importance of the second resolution. In effect, it transforms the first resolution's tentative targets into firm ceilings and, in some ways, ties the hands of the authorizing and revenue committees, and Appropriations Committees, which must comply with the instructions.

The Reagan administration's use of the reconciliation procedures in the first concurrent resolution for fiscal 1982 is the best example of how powerful a device it can be. As noted, the proposed budget cuts were enormous. One possible administration strategy could have been to follow the standard procedures of the budget process and attempt to pass a first resolution with targets that simply assumed that the actual cuts would be made later by the authorizing committees and Appropriations Committees. This, by itself, would have been a significant achievement. It also would have forced the administration to fight for each of the cuts separately as the various authorization and appropriations bills were debated. By using the reconciliation process, the president was able to set a first resolution that reflected his budget priorities and to guarantee that the necessary spending reductions would be made in compliance with those priorities. He achieved it all with essentially one vote. Obviously, this greatly increased the likelihood of the administration's overall success—and the magnitude of the victory.

The reconciliation procedures themselves are relatively simple. A concurrent resolution on the budget contains language that directs one or more committees to make changes in existing law to comply with the targets, or ceilings of that resolution. These instructions are in dollar terms, but the program changes are wholly the responsibility of the relevant authorizing committee or Appropriations Committee, even if assumptions are included by the Budget Committees in their report on the budget resolution or are mentioned during debate. Unlike budget resolutions, reconciliation instructions are made by committee, not by function. If only one committee is specified, it reports a reconciliation bill[3] to its respective house with its recommendations as to how to achieve the required changes. If more than one committee is involved, they submit their recommendations to their respective Budget Committee, which assembles them into a single package without making any substantive changes in the recommendations. If a committee refuses or otherwise fails to make the required recommendations, however, the Budget Committees in certain circumstances can make them in their stead.[4]

Reconciliation directions can be provided to both authorizing committees and Appropriations Committees, even though only action by the latter actually allows the federal government to spend dollars (see chapter 1). However, all reconciliation efforts to date have dealt only with the Authorization Committees. This tactic also ties the hands of the Appropriations Committees without specifically ordering them to do anything, since they cannot provide funds at levels higher than the existing authorizations.

This emphasis on authorizations has led to an unanticipated problem—the inclusion of nonbudget items in reconciliation bills. For example, the fiscal 1983 reconciliation bill reduced the size of the Federal Communications Commission (FCC) from seven to five members; reduced the Interstate Commerce Commission (ICC) from eleven to seven members; and reduced the length of the ICC terms of office from seven to five years.[5] These provisions might not have become law had they been reviewed on their own in a separate piece of legislation, or they might have taken a very different form. Since the Budget Act does not prevent these additions to a reconciliation bill, and because the Budget Committees are specifically prohibited from making any substantive changes in the recommendations from each committee, there are few ways to stop this from occurring.

One tactic tried with mixed success in 1982 was allowing each committee that received reconciliation instructions to bring its bill to the floor individually, or as part of its regular legislation, rather than having the Budget Committees package all of the recommendations into a single omnibus bill. This enabled other members of Congress to look at each bill more closely and prevented them from hiding support or opposition to a specific provision by voting for a large reconciliation package.

As noted earlier, the Budget Act requires that a reconciliation bill from the second concurrent resolution be passed by September 25. There is no deadline included in the act for a reconciliation bill from the first resolution, since reconciliation was not anticipated. The reconciliation bill from the first resolution for fiscal 1981 did not pass until late November 1980, after the second resolution for that year had passed. The reconciliation from the fiscal 1983 first resolution did not pass until mid-August 1982.

Senate debate on a reconciliation bill is limited to twenty hours and is governed by the same rules that apply to its debate on a budget resolution. The rules for House consideration are determined separately in each instance by the Rules Committee.

If reconciliation is ordered, it is the final step in the budget process unless Congress adopts a subsequent budget resolution (see chapter 6), or the president proposes to impound appropriations in some way, as described in the next chapter.

CHAPTER 8

IMPOUNDMENTS

The president is expected to spend the appropriations that Congress passes in a timely manner and according to the priorities Congress expresses. If the president disagrees with either the level of spending or priorities being proposed, he or she has only one option—to veto the bill in its entirety. No individual item within an appropriation can be vetoed and, if two-thirds of each house, voting separately, votes to override the president, the money must be spent as originally intended.

In spite of these provisions, however, Congress generally has assumed that the president does have some spending discretion, for any other interpretation would change the nature of the presidency from "Chief Executive to Chief Clerk."[1] Congress has permitted the president to refuse to spend funds for three reasons: to promote efficient management; to comply with statutory language that allowed such discretion; and to fulfill other constitutionally granted powers, particularly the president's role as commander-in-chief.[2] Decisions not to spend appropriated funds in these circumstances have been relatively noncontroversial and have been made by almost every president.

A fourth reason for presidential impoundments—disagreement with congressional budget policy and spending priorities—has, however, been extraordinarily controversial. It was President Richard Nixon's unprecedented refusal to spend congressionally approved appropriations because he disagreed with the policies they embodied that provided the initial impetus and continued momentum necessary for Congress to create not just impoundment control procedures but the entire budget process as well. Congress found itself without any procedure for dealing with Nixon's continued intransigence on impoundments. The only remedy available was to sue the appropriate cabinet secretary to force expenditure of the appropriations, a tactic that most representatives and senators found cumbersome, time-consuming, and unsatisfactory.

The impoundment control procedures that Congress created not only provided a means to review presidential actions but required such a review. They probably are the most successful of all the provisions of the Budget Act—so much so, in fact, that until 1981 impoundments ceased to be a significant issue.

The Budget Act divides impoundments into two distinct categories. A "deferral" is an executive action that temporarily withholds or otherwise delays the obligation or expenditure of budget authority. A "rescission" is an executive action not to obligate or spend the budget authority at all. If the president wishes to propose either of these two actions, a special message must be sent to the House, the Senate, and to the comptroller general explaining the proposal in detail, including the amount of budget authority to be deferred or reserved; the department or agency to which the budget authority has been allocated and the specific project for which it is intended; and the reasons for the action. In the case of a deferral, the message must state the period of time that the obligation or expenditure of budget authority is to be delayed. The message must also include the estimated fiscal, economic, and budgetary impact of the action and all other pertinent information.[3]

The comptroller general is required to submit a separate report on the proposed action to both the House and the Senate. Besides making an independent judgment on the information submitted by the president, the comptroller general has the power to reclassify a message if it is found incorrectly labeled. Furthermore, if the comptroller general determines that a deferral or rescission is being attempted by the president without Congress being notified of the action, the comptroller general can send a message to Capitol Hill, and Congress will treat it as if it had been submitted by the president.

Rescission and deferral messages are treated quite differently once Congress receives them. A deferral is automatically approved, and the president can delay the obligation or expenditure of the budget authority unless and until either house of Congress passes a specific impoundment resolution disapproving it. There is no time limit for such congressional action. A rescission, on the other hand, must be specifically approved by both houses of Congress within forty-five legislative days after the message is received from the president. If either the House or the Senate disapproves of the proposal or takes no action at all, the president must spend the funds. If Congress disapproves a proposed deferral or rescission, or does not act on a proposed rescission, and the president continues to refuse to spend the funds, the comptroller general can sue in federal court to require the money to be spent.

These provisions take virtually all discretion away from the executive branch on impoundment matters. Congress must be notified of all proposed actions by the president and, if this fails to happen, the comptroller general can inform Congress instead. All actions must receive either the implicit or explicit approval of both the House and the Senate, or the president is forced to spend the funds as Congress intended. Finally, the comptroller general is given the authority to bring a legal action if the president continues to refuse to spend the funds as directed.

Until the Reagan administration took office, these procedures were so successful that virtually all controversy surrounding presidential impoundments had been eliminated. In 1981, however, a number of proposals to allow the president to delay or refuse to spend funds without congressional approval again were proposed.

The motivation was the unwillingness of some members of Congress to go on record and vote for additional spending cuts as requested by the president, even though these members supported the cuts. Since existing impoundment control procedures would have forced such a vote, some thought was given to amending the law to permit a percentage of a program's funds to be withheld by the president, thus eliminating the need for Congress to take any responsibility. These proposals were not voted on, however.

Another controversy arose over deferrals when President Reagan proposed additional spending cuts that Congress did not include in the first continuing resolution for fiscal 1982. Since the level of spending in the bill was greater than the president wanted, OMB announced that the president would defer some spending in excess of the September 24 level until the continuing resolution expired on November 20. (Presumably the final appropriations would be enacted by then, and the spending level would be closer to the president's wishes.) But many of the deferrals were not formally sent to Congress, which was a violation of the Budget Act. Congress did not force the issue, however, and the funds either were unspent or were spent at a slower rate until later in the year when the appropriations were enacted.

Rescission and deferral messages are handled jointly by the Budget and Appropriations Committees in the Senate but only by the Appropriations Committee in the House. Floor consideration in the Senate on an impoundment resolution or rescission bill is limited to ten hours of debate, with debate on any amendment to a rescission bill limited to two hours. Debate in the House is limited to two hours, with amendments to rescission bills considered under the five-minute rule. In both the Senate and the House, no amendments are allowed to impoundment resolutions, which must be voted on as presented.

Congressional consideration of presidential impoundments is the final step in the budget process. It provides both the president and Congress the opportunity to make adjustments in the budget after it has been approved if events occur that differ from the assumptions on which the budget was based. The new procedures have eliminated the president's ability to act unilaterally in these matters but not the ability to propose changes.

PART TWO

THE FEDERAL BUDGET

CHAPTER 9

OVERVIEW

This section is a technical guide to the federal budget. Chapters 9 through 14 describe in detail the different budget documents and how to use them. These chapters also explain how to read and interpret the various tables contained in those documents.

The five executive branch budget documents, which are produced by OMB, are clearly partisan in nature and are intended to put the president's program in the best possible light. If used correctly, however, they also can serve as a source of independent, objective information on federal spending and taxing. The five presidential budget documents include the most detailed information ordinarily available on federal activities. As noted in chapter 3, Congress uses these documents more than any other source of budget data, and they serve as the starting point for most congressional deliberations. The following pages describe the five documents.

The Budget of the United States Government

This is the basic budget document. It includes the president's budget message; an explanation of the economic policy and projections on which the budget is based; descriptions of the spending and taxing proposals by both function and department; and summary tables that present the budget historically and according to certain accounting and budget principles.

The *Budget* is the most useful of the five presidential budget documents since it displays the information in a form that permits comparison with previous years and contains just enough detail to make the contrast useful.

The Budget of the United States Government—Appendix

The *Appendix* is the most detailed budget document. It lists, by department, the proposed text of appropriations language and the activities and financing of each program under the jurisdiction of that department.

The *Appendix* is the size of a large city telephone directory with print almost as small, and the extraordinary detail it contains is not appropriate for most budget users. The *Appendix* cannot easily be used to answer questions about the aggregate funding levels for an agency or department, or for a functional analysis of federal activities. To look beyond the overall total to individual line items, however, this is the only suitable document.

Major Themes and Additional Budget Details

Major Themes provides a detailed explanation and justification for most of the proposals that constitute the president's budget. In the past, a description of the program that would be affected, proposed change, rationale, and the "effects of the proposed change" have been included for each item.

Major Themes is a highly partisan presentation that must be used carefully. The information provided is only a brief statement of the administration's position; it is not intended to be a complete discussion of the pros and cons of each issue.

The United States Budget In Brief

This document is a less technical presentation of the basic *Budget of the United States Government*. Although it provides summary and historical tables and multicolored graphs, it is not detailed enough to permit much independent analysis.

Special Analyses, Budget of the United States Government

Special Analyses contains eleven separate reports that look at federal spending in ways that cut across several budget functions or involve more than one department—for example, "Aid to State and Local Governments" and "Research and Development" activities. The analyses also contain "alternative views" of the budget, including the current services estimates and national income accounts.

The special analyses reports must be used carefully since the information is not necessarily presented objectively. In addition, much of the data are presented in narrative form, making independent judgments difficult.

CHAPTER 10

THE BUDGET OF THE UNITED STATES GOVERNMENT

The *Budget of the United States Government* (hereafter referred to as the *Budget*) is the most useful of the five documents submitted by the president to Congress. Besides describing the administration's program in detail, the *Budget* contains sections that break down the spending plan by both budget function and agency. The document also includes extensive summary tables. This information permits an independent analysis of the program presented by the administration. For most budget users, the *Budget* is the first place to look.

Like all executive branch budget documents, the *Budget* is partly a partisan policy document and partly an objective accounting statement. Besides the administration's program, the fiscal 1984 budget also contains the final figures for fiscal 1982 and the most recent estimate for fiscal 1983, the two previous budget years. The *Budget* can, therefore, be used as a neutral base to evaluate administration claims. Doing so eliminates the need to rely on the administration's own analysis, which is presented in the narrative accompanying each section.

To research a specific activity, there are two main places to look for information. First, part 5 describes the president's program by "function"—the budget authority, outlays, loans, loan guarantees, and tax expenditures intended to meet a particular national need. For information about overall functions, for example, Health, National Defense, or Transportation, this is the section to review.[1] Second, part 8 displays the president's proposals by agency. This section contains information about particular programs.

The following pages describe the nine parts of the *Budget*; explain how to read the tables in each part; and warn about the pitfalls to avoid.

Part 1: The Budget Message of the President

This section presents the president's program in minimal detail and with rhetoric that puts it in the best light. Although based on the information presented in later sections, the budget message is largely a public relations tool. It is the official message that accompanied the budget when it was sent to Congress.

Part 2: Economic Assumptions and the Budget Outlook

This section is the president's view of the economy and a brief summary of the aggregate budget proposal. It also includes the fiscal policy the administration thinks necessary in light of economic conditions; longer-range projections of the state of the economy; and the budgets the president plans to work toward achieving over the next three years.

This section is extremely important to understanding the spending estimates and projections in each of the functions presented in part 5 of the *Budget*, since, as noted in chapter 1, many of them are dependent on the economic assumptions presented. In 1980, for example, actual federal spending was $48 billion higher than the original budget estimate of January 1979, with over half the increase directly attributable to economic conditions that were different from those originally assumed in the budget.

Most of the information presented in this part of the *Budget* is self-explanatory. Several tables should, however, be looked at carefully.

Table 6 presents the economic data on which the fiscal 1983 budget proposal is based. Note the following points (numbers 1–5 in this list correspond to 1–5 in table 6):

1.   All information is presented on a calendar year (January 1–December 31) basis, as is customary for economic statistics. This is different from the spending and tax estimates in the *Budget*, which are presented on a fiscal year basis (October 1–September 30).

2.   The table is in billions of dollars.

3.   Many of the figures in this table are in percentages, not dollars.

4.   Figures are presented in both current and constant dollars for purposes of comparison.[2]

5.   These are the actual figures for 1981 and the preliminary figures for 1982. However, the figures for 1983 and 1984 are only forecasts of probable economic conditions that are consistent with the administration's budget proposals.

TABLE 6

SHORT-RANGE ECONOMIC FORECAST

(Calendar years; dollar amounts in billions)

Item	Actual 1981	Forecast 1982 [1]	Forecast 1983	Forecast 1984
Major economic indicators:				
Gross national product, percent change, fourth quarter over fourth quarter:				
Current dollars	9.6	3.3	8.8	9.2
Constant (1972) dollars	0.7	−1.2	3.1	4.0
GNP deflator (percent change, fourth quarter over fourth quarter)	8.9	4.6	5.6	5.0
Consumer Price Index (percent change, fourth quarter over fourth quarter) [2]	9.4	4.4	5.0	4.4
Unemployment rate (percent, fourth quarter) [3]	8.1	10.5	10.4	9.5
Annual economic assumptions:				
Gross national product:				
Current dollars:				
Amount	2,938	3,058	3,262	3,566
Percent change, year over year	11.6	4.1	6.7	9.3
Constant (1972) dollars:				
Amount	1,503	1,476	1,496	1,555
Percent change, year over year	1.9	−1.8	1.4	3.9
Incomes:				
Personal income	2,416	2,570	2,727	2,935
Wages and salaries	1,494	1,560	1,640	1,780
Corporate profits	232	175	177	206
Price level:				
GNP deflator:				
Level (1972 = 100), annual average	195.5	207.2	218.1	229.4
Percent change, year over year	9.4	6.0	5.2	5.2
Consumer Price Index: [2]				
Level (1967 = 100), annual average	272.3	288.6	302.9	316.8
Percent change, year over year	10.3	6.0	4.9	4.6
Unemployment rates:				
Total, annual average [3]	7.5	9.5	10.7	9.9
Insured, annual average [4]	3.5	4.7	5.3	4.7
Federal pay raise, October (percent) [5]	4.8	4.0		6.1
Interest rate, 91-day Treasury bills (percent) [6]	14.1	10.7	8.0	7.9
Interest rate, 10-year Treasury notes (percent)	13.9	13.0	10.2	9.8

[1] Preliminary actual data.
[2] CPI for urban wage earners and clerical workers. Two versions of the CPI are now published. The index shown here is that currently used, as required by law, in calculating automatic cost-of-living increases for indexed Federal programs. The figures in this table reflect the actual CPI for December 1982, released January 21, 1983, which was 0.7% lower than had been projected; consequently, the cost-of-living adjustments estimated in the budget are higher than the actual adjustments will be.
[3] Percent of total labor force, including armed forces stationed in the U.S.
[4] This indicator measures unemployment under State regular unemployment insurance as a percentage of covered employment under that program. It does not include recipients of extended benefits under that program.
[5] General schedule pay raises become effective in October—the first month of the fiscal year. Thus, the October 1984 pay raise will set new pay scales that will be in effect during fiscal year 1985. The October 1981 pay raise for military personnel was 14.3%.
[6] Average rate on new issues within period, on a bank discount basis. These projections assume, by convention, that interest rates decline with the rate of inflation. They do not represent a forecast of interest rates.

Table 7 is presented in the same form as table 6, "Short-range Economic Assumptions," with one important exception—*the longer-range assumptions for 1985 to 1988 are not forecasts of probable economic conditions*. Instead, they are projections that assume steady progress in reducing unemployment and inflation consistent with the administration's economic goals.

Part 3: Budget Program and Trends

In past years, this section has dealt primarily with a number of technical budget issues. This year, however, the administration is using it to discuss and illustrate its entire fiscal 1984 proposal. This is the most succinct description of the overall program proposal by the president. However, the section must be used carefully since the information is not necessarily objective. All claims and comparisons should be reviewed carefully.

Keeping this in mind, the reader can use this section to review the budget impact of the individual parts of the 1984 budget proposal. Each of the following sections contains both a narrative description and at least one table: *The Current Services Outlook; Sources of the Structural Deficit; The Inherited Budgetary Imbalance; Redirection of Fiscal Policy Launched in 1981; The 1984 Budget Recommendations: A Comprehensive Program to Close the Structural Deficit;* and *Outlook for Closing the Structural Deficit with the 1984 Budget Plan.*

Part 4: Budget Receipts

This section treats revenues as if they comprised a separate budget function. Besides providing the aggregate level of receipts, this section breaks totals down into their various sources and explains the probable impact of any new revenue proposals the administration has included in the budget.

TABLE 7

LONG-RANGE ECONOMIC ASSUMPTIONS

(Calendar years; dollar amounts in billions)

	Assumptions			
	1985	1986	1987	1988
Major economic indicators:				
Gross national product, percent change, fourth quarter over fourth quarter:				
Current dollars	9.0	8.7	8.7	8.6
Constant (1972) dollars	4.0	4.0	4.0	4.0
GNP deflator (percent change, fourth quarter over fourth quarter)	4.8	4.5	4.5	4.4
Consumer Price Index (percent change, fourth quarter over fourth quarter) [1]	4.7	4.5	4.5	4.4
Unemployment rate (percent, fourth quarter) [3]	8.5	7.8	7.0	6.2
Annual economic assumptions:				
Gross national product:				
Current dollars:				
Amount	3,890	4,232	4,599	4,995
Percent change, year over year	9.1	8.8	8.7	8.6
Constant (1972) dollars:				
Amount	1,617	1,682	1,749	1,819
Percent change, year over year	4.0	4.0	4.0	4.0
Incomes:				
Personal income	3,142	3,377	3,661	3,956
Wages and salaries	1,921	2,090	2,281	2,483
Corporate profits	246	296	316	329
Price level:				
GNP deflator:				
Level (1972 = 100), annual average	240.6	251.7	263.0	274.7
Percent change, year over year	4.9	4.6	4.5	4.4
Consumer Price Index: [1]				
Level (1967 = 100), annual average	331.4	346.6	362.2	378.3
Percent change, year over year	4.6	4.6	4.5	4.4
Unemployment rates:				
Total, annual average [2]	8.9	8.1	7.3	6.5
Insured, annual average [3]	4.2	3.8	3.5	3.2
Federal pay raise, October (percent) [4]	6.0	5.7	5.6	5.5
Interest rate, 91-day Treasury bills (percent) [5]	7.4	6.8	6.5	6.1
Interest rate, 10-year Treasury notes (percent)	9.0	8.0	7.4	6.7

[1] CPI for urban wage earners and clerical workers. Two versions of the CPI are now published. The index shown here is that currently used, as required by law, in calculating automatic cost-of-living increases for indexed Federal programs. The manner in which this index measures housing costs will change significantly in 1985.

[2] Percent of total labor force, including armed forces stationed in the U.S.

[3] This indicator measures unemployment under State regular unemployment insurance as a percentage of covered employment under that program. It does not include recipients of extended benefits under that program.

[4] General schedule pay raises become effective in October—the first month of the fiscal year. Thus, the October 1985 pay raise will set new pay scales that will be in effect during fiscal year 1986.

[5] Average rate on new issues within period, on a bank discount basis. These projections assume, by convention, that interest rates decline with the rate of inflation. They do not represent a forecast of interest rates.

Reprinted from the 1984 Budget, p. 2–10.

Table 8 should be examined carefully when reviewing part 4 of the *Budget*. Note the following points:

1. The table is in billions of dollars.
2. The totals for fiscal 1982 are the actual figures for that year, but those for fiscal 1983 are only the most recent estimates available. The figures for fiscal 1984 include changes that already have been enacted into law and *the estimated impact of all new administration revenue proposals*. The figures for fiscal 1985 and 1986 are estimates of the receipts from current law plus the effects of the revenue changes for fiscal 1984 that the administration has proposed and is assuming will be passed. Since all of these factors are subject to change, the totals for these two years can be considered rough estimates.

TABLE 8

BUDGET RECEIPTS BY SOURCE

(In billions of dollars)

Source	1982 actual	1983 estimate	1984 estimate	1985 estimate	1986 estimate
Individual income taxes	297.7	285.2	295.6	317.9	358.6
Corporation income taxes	49.2	35.3	51.8	60.5	74.0
Social insurance taxes and contributions	201.5	210.3	242.9	275.5	304.9
Excise taxes	36.3	37.3	40.4	40.8	74.8
Estate and gift taxes	8.0	6.1	5.9	5.6	5.0
Customs duties	8.9	8.8	9.1	9.4	9.7
Miscellaneous receipts	16.2	14.5	14.0	14.5	14.8
Total, budget receipts	**617.8**	**597.5**	**659.7**	**724.3**	**841.9**

Reprinted from the 1984 *Budget*, p. 4–3.

Part 5: Meeting National Needs: The Federal Program by Function

This is the largest and, for most readers, most important part of the *Budget* since it is presented by function[3]—the same format Congress uses for the first and second concurrent resolutions on the budget. Comparisons between the spending priorities of the president and Congress can, therefore, be made using this section.

Each of the nineteen functions begins with a brief "National Needs Statement"—the administration's goals in that area of federal activity—and continues with a narrative explanation of the administration's program. Great care must be taken when reading this section since an administration puts its proposals in the best light, and the level of spending on a program for this year often is compared to whatever previous year will make it look best. For example, if all programs except one are being compared to fiscal 1983, but a particular program is compared to fiscal 1982, there must be some reason for that different comparison. In addition, some comparisons may be made using budget authority when outlays are really the important figure to be looking at. It is important to refrain from taking the narrative description of a function at face value.

Each function contains several different tables that make it relatively easy to verify an administration's claims. Table 9 is the typical main spending table and the key points to be aware of are as follows:

1.　Some functions have separate tables for budget authority and outlays. Other functions, such as this one, combine the two into one table. It is essential not to confuse them.

2.　The table is in millions of dollars.

3.　The columns display the totals over a five-year period. *The third column, (1984), represents the administration's proposed budget and, therefore, is the most important.* The first column, (1982), reflects actual spending for that year. The second column, (1983), is the most recent estimate of the spending that will occur in the current fiscal year. The last two columns, (1985 and 1986), simply are projections by the administration of what it may do in those fiscal years and are not final decisions.

4.　Totals and subtotals are indicated by double lines.

TABLE 9

NATIONAL NEED: INCREASING BASIC SCIENTIFIC KNOWLEDGE AND USE OF SPACE

(Functional code 250; in millions of dollars)

Major missions and programs	1982 actual	1983 estimate	1984 estimate	1985 estimate	1986 estimate
BUDGET AUTHORITY					
General science and basic research:					
National Science Foundation programs	1,006	1,099	1,297	1,297	1,297
Energy-related general science programs	529	535	645	759	744
Subtotal, general science and basic research	1,535	1,635	1,943	2,057	2,042
Space research and technology:					
Space flight	3,601	4,109	4,049	3,699	3,058
Space science, applications, and technology	1,392	1,568	1,638	1,819	1,828
Supporting space activities	544	610	830	836	816
Subtotal, space research and technology	5,537	6,287	6,517	6,354	5,702
Deductions for offsetting receipts	−10	−9	−9	−9	−9
Total, budget authority	7,063	7,912	8,451	8,403	7,735
OUTLAYS					
General science and basic research:					
National Science Foundation programs	1,099	1,066	1,231	1,320	1,339
Energy-related general science programs	507	547	634	733	717
Subtotal, general science and basic research	1,607	1,613	1,865	2,053	2,056
Space research and technology:					
Space flight	3,543	4,034	4,028	3,762	3,193
Space science, applications, and technology	1,457	1,517	1,601	1,768	1,808
Supporting space activities	473	604	766	826	822
Subtotal, space research and technology	5,473	6,155	6,395	6,356	5,823
Deductions for offsetting receipts	−10	−9	−9	−9	−9
Total, outlays	7,070	7,759	8,250	8,401	7,871
ADDENDUM					
Off-budget Federal entity:					
Federal Financing Bank:					
Supporting space activities:					
Budget authority	146	205	37		
Outlays	120	175	−140	−90	−91

Reprinted from the 1984 *Budget*, p. 5–28.

Table 10 is a typical table showing the credit programs in each function. Note the following key points:

1. The table shows the outlay equivalent of the direct loans and guaranteed loans.
2. The table is in millions of dollars.
3. The first column, (1982), contains the actual figures for fiscal

TABLE 10

CREDIT PROGRAMS: AGRICULTURE

2 (In millions of dollars)

	Actual 1982	Estimate			
3		1983	1984	1985	1986
Direct loans:					
Commodity price support and related loans (CCC):					
New obligations	11,500	11,877	8,040	5,600	5,600
Net outlays	6,325	4,382	−2,025	358	1,300
Outstandings	12,484	16,867	14,842	15,200	16,500
Agricultural Credit Insurance Fund (FmHA):					
New obligations [1]	4,199	4,264	3,979	4,065	4,012
Net outlays	−241	−420	−132	....	....
Outstandings	795	375	243	243	243
Agricultural credit insurance fund of FmHA (loans held by FFB): [1]					
Net outlays	1,055	835	−104	−163	−216
Outstandings	23,412	24,247	24,143	23,979	23,764
Total, direct loans:					
New obligations	15,699	16,141	12,019	9,665	9,612
Net outlays	7,139	4,797	−2,261	195	1,084
Outstandings	36,691	41,488	39,227	39,422	40,506
Guaranteed loans:					
Export credit (CCC):					
New commitments	1,551	4,800	3,000	3,000	3,000
Net change	645	3,389	−412	−126	−500
Outstandings	2,650	6,038	5,626	5,500	5,000
Agricultural and emergency credit (FmHA):					
New commitments	57	131	106	106	106
Net change	−187	−32	−49	862	−1,075
Outstandings	1,132	1,100	1,051	1,913	838
Total, guaranteed loans:					
New commitments	1,608	4,931	3,106	3,106	3,106
Net change	458	3,357	−461	735	−1,575
Outstandings	3,782	7,138	6,677	7,413	5,838
Total credit budget (new obligations and new commitments)	**1** 17,307	21,072	15,125	12,771	12,718

[1] The direct lending activities of the Farmers Home Administration (FmHA) are financed by the Federal Financing Bank (FFB). Certificates of beneficial ownership (CBO's) are issued by the FmHA. According to law, these certificates are backed by loans that the agency continues to service. FmHA guarantees the CBO's, sells them to the FFB, and repurchases them upon maturity. FFB net outlays for REA represent acquisition of CBO's less repurchases by FmHA. Increases in the volume of sales of CBO's are added to FFB direct loan outstandings, while the FmHA's direct loan outstandings decrease by the amount of CBO's sold to the FFB.

Reprinted from the 1984 Budget, p. 5–52.

1982. The second column, (1983), contains the best current estimate of the credit activity that will occur in fiscal 1983. The third column, (1984), contains the president's proposal for fiscal 1984. The fourth and fifth columns, (1985 and 1986), do not represent actual proposals but are projections of current policies to those years.

Part 6: Perspectives on the Budget

This section explains a number of technical aspects of the budget as well as several other subjects related to but not part of the budget itself. These discussions can be helpful in understanding the constraints on the budget and the full scope of federal fiscal activities. The following topics are included: *Relationship of Budget Authority to Outlays; Fiscal Activities Outside the Federal Budget; Federal Budget for Capital Expenditures; Budget Funds and the Federal Debt; The Increase in Total 1982 Outlays Over the March 1981 Budget Estimate; Comparison of Relatively Uncontrollable Outlays and of Receipts;* and *Allocation of Windfall Profit Tax Receipts.*

Part 7: The Budget System and Concepts

This section is a brief explanation of the executive and congressional budget processes and of several key concepts and definitions used in federal budgeting. Chapters 1 through 8 of this book explain in greater detail much of the information provided in this part.

Part 8: The Federal Program By Agency and Account

This section is an alternative presentation of the information included in part 5 of the *Budget*, where it was displayed by function. No narrative explanation is provided, and all programs of each department and agency are presented in a single table, regardless of the functions in which they otherwise are found. Table 11 is an example of a typical table found in part 8. Note the following key points:

1. Budget authority (BA) and outlays (O) are listed in the same table. Budget authority will always be in bold type, outlays in roman type.

2. The table is in thousands of dollars.

3. Activities within the same department or agency often are distributed among different functions. In this table, Fair Housing Assistance is listed in function 751 (a subfunction of function 750: Administration of Justice), while the New

TABLE 11

BUDGET ACCOUNTS LISTING, DEPARTMENT OF HOUSING AND URBAN DEVELOPMENT

2

BUDGET ACCOUNTS LISTING (in thousands of dollars)—Continued

Account and functional code		1982 actual	1983 estimate	1984 estimate
New Community Development Corporation—Con.				
Public Enterprise Funds:				
New communities fund	451			
Authority to borrow, permanent, indefinite	BA	18,587	32,396	26,100
				L —26,100
Contract authority, permanent, indefinite **1**	BA	12,366	77,275	....
Outlays	O	15,983	37,122	30,100
				L —30,100
Total New communities fund	BA	30,953	109,671	....
	O	15,983	37,122	....
Total Federal funds New Community Development Corporation	BA	30,071	109,671	.... **4**
	O	16,901	38,154	....
Policy Development and Research				
Federal funds				
General and Special Funds:				
Research and technology	451			
Appropriation, current	BA	20,000	18,000	....
				K 18,000
Outlays	O	26,699	25,440	22,000
Total Research and technology	BA	20,000	18,000	18,000
	O	26,699	25,440	22,000
Fair Housing and Equal Opportunity				
Federal funds				
General and Special Funds:				
Fair housing assistance **3** 751				
Appropriation, current	BA	5,016	5,700	4,700
Outlays	O	2,360	10,800	6,400
Management and Administration				
Federal funds				
General and Special Funds:				
Salaries and expenses, Including transfer of funds:				
(Community development)	451			
(Appropriation, current)	BA	194,800	201,660	191,350
(Outlays)	O	196,152	205,056	191,591
(Public assistance and other income supplements)	604			
(Appropriation, current)	BA	102,720	82,578	87,782
(Outlays)	O	103,433	83,969	87,893
(Federal law enforcement activities)	751			
(Appropriation, current)	BA	21,980	23,262	23,975
(Outlays)	O	22,132	23,654	24,005
Total Salaries and expenses, Including transfer of funds	BA	319,500	307,500	303,107
	O	321,717	312,679	303,489

K Additional authorizing legislation required.
L Legislative action required.

Reprinted from the 1984 *Budget*, p. 8–102.

Communities Fund is listed in function 451 (a subfunction of function 450: Community and Regional Development). Appendix D of this book provides a description of the nineteen functions and the major programs contained in them. Chapter 1 of this book contains a full explanation of budget functions.

4. A dotted line indicates that the program was started in a later budget and did not exist previously, or it was started in an earlier budget and no longer is being funded.

Part 9: Summary Tables

This section consists of twenty-three tables that display in a more concise manner the information initially presented in the earlier sections of the *Budget.*

Tables 1 through 11 in part 9 are relatively short summaries of the budget as a whole. They are as follows:

Table 1: Budget Summary

Table 2: Budget Receipts by Source and Budget Outlays by Agency, 1982–88

Table 3: Budget Outlays by Function, 1982–88—This table summarizes part 5.

Table 4: Budget Authority by Agency, 1982–88—This table summarizes part 8.

Table 5: Budget Authority by Function, 1982–88—This table summarizes part 5.

Table 6: Budget Authority and Outlays Available through Current Action by Congress—This table shows the amount of budget authority and outlays, by department or agency, that Congress must take some action on for the funds to be spent. These are the "relatively controllable" funds in each agency.

Table 7: Relation of Budget Authority to Outlays—This table combines the "relatively controllable" funds from table 6 with the "relatively uncontrollable" funds to show the proportion of each in the totals for budget authority and outlays and how budget authority and outlays relate to each other.

Table 8: *Obligations Incurred Net*—This table shows the actual amount of budget authority that has been or will be obligated by each agency.

Table 9: *Balances of Budget Authority*—This table shows the budget authority already provided to each agency that has not yet resulted in outlays. "Obligated" refers to budget authority already committed to a particular purpose and for which the contracts committing the spending have been signed. "Unobligated" refers to budget authority that has been committed but for which contracts have not yet been signed.

Table 10: *Full-time Equivalent of Total Federal Civilian Employment in the Executive Branch*

Table 11: *Budget Financing and Debt*

Tables 12 through 14 provide more detail on the information provided in tables 1, 2, and 3. These three tables are in millions of dollars. They are as follows:

Table 12: *Budget Receipts by Source*

Table 13: *Offsetting Receipts by Type*

Table 14: *Outlays by Function and Agency*

Table 15: *Legislative Proposals for Major New and Expanded Programs in the 1984 Budget, Projection of Costs*—This is a five-year estimate of the costs of all legislative changes proposed in the fiscal 1984 budget submitted by the president. Estimates do not reflect any changes in the scope and quality of programs as they are implemented that may have some impact on the amount eventually to be spent. In addition, these estimates do not necessarily include reductions in the costs of other programs that may result from the adoption and implementation of the new proposals, nor in the amounts to be requested for them in future years.

Table 16: *New Direct Loan Obligations By Agency*

Table 17: New Loan Guarantee Commitments By Agency

Table 18 through 24 provide some historical perspective and allow trends to be seen easily by comparing the data from tables 1 through 17 with data from previous budgets. As noted, each of these tables is based on a different amount of money, so great care should be taken when using them. The tables are as follows:

Table 18: Controllability of Budget Outlays 1974–84 (In billions of dollars)

Table 19: Budget Receipts by Source, 1974–84 (In millions of dollars)

Table 20: Budget Outlays by Function, 1974–84 (In millions of dollars)

Table 21: Federal Transactions in the National Income Accounts, 1973–84 (In billions of dollars)

Table 22: Federal Finances and the Gross National Product, 1965–84 (In billions of dollars)—Percentages also are included.

Table 23: Composition of Budget Outlays in Current and Constant (Fiscal Year 1972) Prices: 1963–86 (In millions of dollars)

Table 24: Budget Receipts and Outlays, 1789–1986 (In millions of dollars)

CHAPTER 11

THE BUDGET OF THE UNITED STATES GOVERNMENT—APPENDIX

The *Budget of the United States Government–Appendix* (hereafter referred to as the *Appendix*) is the most detailed of the five presidential budget documents. In fact, it provides more detail than necessary for most budget users. For each department and agency, the *Appendix* includes, by appropriation account, the following: the proposed text of appropriation language; a detailed expenditure and financing schedule; new legislative proposals, if any; an explanation of the work to be performed and the funds needed; and a schedule of permanent personnel positions.

Furthermore, the *Appendix* includes proposed general provisions applicable to the appropriations of entire agencies or groups of agencies; supplemental and rescission proposals; the president's recommendations for executive, legislative, and judicial salaries; and budget estimates for off-budget federal entities.[1]

The remainder of this chapter describes the seven parts of the *Appendix*, explains how to read the tables in each part, and warns about pitfalls to avoid.

Part 1: Detailed Budget Estimates

This is the most important part of the *Appendix*. Each appropriation account in every department and agency is explained with the following four elements:

1. *Proposed Text of Appropriations Language*

The appropriation language proposed by the president for fiscal 1984 is printed as noted in the following paragraph under the account title, "Office of the Secretary," for example. The items enclosed within the bold-type brackets "[ ]" are proposed to be deleted from the existing fiscal 1983 appropriation. The material in italic type is proposed substitute or additional language. At the end of the paragraph, printed in italic type in parentheses, are citations to any relevant authorizing legislation, and to the appropriations act from which the basic text of the proposed 1984 language has been taken.

Department of Agriculture, Office of the Secretary

For necessary expenses of the Office of the Secretary of Agriculture, including not to exceed $75,000 for employment under 5 U.S.C. 3109, [$3,884,000] *$5,045,000: Provided,* That not to exceed $8,000 of this amount shall be available for official reception and representation expenses, not otherwise provided for, as determined by the Secretary. *(5 U.S.C. 5901; 7 U.S.C. 450c–450g, 2201–06, 2210–13, 2221, 2231, 2232, 2235; 42 U.S.C. 2000d; Public Law 97–370 making appropriations for Agriculture, Rural Development, and Related Agencies, 1983.)**

2. *Program and Financing Schedule*

Table 12 is the basic table in the *Appendix.* Note the following points:

   1.   Everything in this section is in terms of budget authority. The elements of this section vary for each appropriation. The final figure, in bold type, is the total budget authority being requested.

   2.   The table is in thousands of dollars.

   3.   The first column, (1982), contains the actual figures for fiscal 1982. The second column, (1983), contains the best current estimate of the spending that will occur in fiscal 1983, and the third column, (1984), contains the president's proposal for fiscal 1984.

   4.   This section refers to the proposed appropriation. In most cases the appropriation and budget authority will be equal.

   5.   This section refers to outlays.

   6.   The outlays projected for fiscal 1984 always are listed on this line.

   7.   These are computer codes that can be ignored.

---

*Reprinted from Office of Management and Budget, *Budget of the United States Government, Fiscal Year 1984, Appendix* (Washington, D.C.: Government Printing Office, 1983) p. I–E1.

TABLE 12

PROGRAM AND FINANCING

Program and Financing (in thousands of dollars) **2**

Identification code 12–0115–0–1–352 **3**	1982 actual	1983 est.	1984 est.
Program by activities:			
Direct program:			
1. Program and policy direction and coordination:			
(a) Office of the Secretary and Deputy Secretary	2,294	2,361	2,387
(b) Under/Assistant Secretaries	1,947	2,334	2,658
2. Regulatory hearings and decisions	521	....	....
Total direct program	4,762	4,695	5,045
Reimbursable program:			
1. Program and policy direction and coordination:			
(a) Office of the Secretary and Deputy Secretary	144	265	265
(b) Under/Assistant Secretaries	856	371	371
2. Regulatory hearings and decisions	22	....	....
Total reimbursable programs	1,022	636	636
7 ⑩ **10.00** Total obligations	5,784	5,331	5,681
Financing:			
11.00 Offsetting collections from: Federal funds	−1,022	−636	−636
25.00 Unobligated balance lapsing	237	....	....
39.00 **Budget authority**	**4,999**	**4,695** **1** ⑤ 5,045
Budget authority:			
40.00 Appropriation	4,999	3,884	5,045
42.00 Transferred from other accounts	....	493	....
43.00 **Appropriation (adjusted)**	**4,999**	**4,377**	**5,045**
44.20 **Supplemental for civilian pay raises**	....	**318**	....
Relation of obligations to outlays:			
71.00 Obligations incurred, net	4,762	4,695	5,045
72.40 Obligated balance, start of year	1,286	1,024	1,101
74.40 Obligated balance, end of year	−1,024	−1,101	−1,101
77.00 Adjustments in expired accounts	203	....	....
90.00 Outlays, excluding pay raise supplemental	5,227	4,304 **6** ⑤ 5,041
91.20 Outlays from civilian pay raise supplemental	....	314	4

Note.—Excludes $673 thousand in 1983 and $607 thousand in 1984 for activities transferred to Standard Level User Charges, Department of Agriculture. The comparable amount for 1982 ($378 thousand) is included above.

Reprinted from the 1984 *Appendix*, p. I–E1.

3. *Narrative Statement of Program and Performance*

Narrative statements such as the following present the objectives of the program and purposes of the appropriation.

> The Office of the Secretary covers the overall planning, coordination, and administration of the Department's programs.

> *Program and policy direction and coordination.*— This includes the Secretary, Deputy Secretary, Under Secretaries, Assistant Secretaries, and their immediate staffs who provide top policy guidance for the Department; maintain relationships with agricultural organizations and others in the development of farm programs; and provide liaison with the Executive Office of the President and Members of Congress on all matters pertaining to agricultural policy.[*]

4. *Object Classification Schedules*

The "object classes" in table 13 indicate the nature of the things proposed to be purchased. Note the following points:

1. The table is in thousands of dollars.
2. The first column, (1982), shows the actual figures for fiscal 1982. The second column, (1983), shows the best current estimate of the spending that will occur in fiscal 1983, and the third column, (1984), shows the president's proposal for fiscal 1984.
3. These are computer codes that can be ignored.

---

[*]Reprinted from the 1984 Appendix, p. I–E1.

TABLE 13

OBJECT CLASSIFICATION

1

Object Classification (in thousands of dollars)

Identification code 12–0115–0–1–352 **2**	1982 actual	1983 est.	1984 est.
3 Direct obligations:			
Personnel compensation:			
11.1 Full-time permanent	2,632	3,009	3,246
11.3 Other than full-time permanent	160	146	146
11.5 Other personnel compensation	69	52	52
11.9 Total personnel compensation	2,861	3,207	3,444
12.1 Personnel benefits: Civilian	251	286	309
13.0 Benefits for former personnel	4	8	10
21.0 Travel and transportation of persons	279	322	342
22.0 Transportation of things	10	2	2
23.1 Standard level user charges	378	....	....
23.2 Communications, utilities, and other rent	432	327	320
24.0 Printing and reproduction	162	140	249
25.0 Other services	242	289	221
26.0 Supplies and materials	131	99	126
31.0 Equipment	12	15	22
99.0 Subtotal, direct obligations	4,762	4,695	5,045
Reimbursable obligations:			
11.1 Personnel compensation: Full-time permanent	656	406	406
12.1 Personnel benefits: Civilian	69	39	39
21.0 Travel and transportation of persons	32	45	45
22.0 Transportation of things	2	....	....
23.2 Communications, utilities, and other rent	55	34	34
24.0 Printing and reproduction	16	17	17
25.0 Other services	158	80	80
26.0 Supplies and materials	9	15	15
31.0 Equipment	25	....	....
99.0 Subtotal, reimbursable obligations	1,022	636	636
99.9 Total obligations	5,784	5,331	5,681

Reprinted from the 1984 *Appendix*, p. I–E1.

A personnel summary for the account, as is displayed in table 14, usually follows the object classification schedule. Note the following points:

1. The table is in actual numbers.
2. This is the number of full-time permanent positions expected to be filled, not necessarily the maximum number authorized.
3. "ES" refers to "senior executive service."

TABLE 14

PERSONNEL SUMMARY

Total number of full-time permanent positions..........	121	102	102 **1,2**
Total compensable workyears:			
Full-time equivalent employment	101	93	93
Full-time equivalent of overtime and holiday hours	4	4	4
Average ES salary **3**	$58,500	$63,220	$63,220
Average GS grade...	9.52	9.87	9.87
Average GS salary...	$26,284	$27,335	$27,335
Average salary of ungraded positions	$21,289	$22,141	$22,141

Reprinted from the 1984 *Appendix*, p. I–E1.

Part 2: Schedules of Permanent Positions

This part contains detailed schedules of the permanent positions in each department and agency. There is one basic table for each office within each agency (see table 15). Note the following points in table 15:

1. The table is in actual numbers.
2. The first column, (1982), is the actual number of permanent positions for fiscal 1982. The second column, (1983), is the best current estimate for fiscal 1983, and the third column, (1984), is the number of permanent positions proposed for fiscal 1984.
3. "ES" refers to "senior executive service."
4. The number refers to the employment grade.

TABLE 15

DEPARTMENT OF THE INTERIOR, OFFICE OF SURFACE MINING RECLAMATION AND ENFORCEMENT

CONSOLIDATED SCHEDULE OF PERMANENT POSI-
TIONS, THE OFFICE OF SURFACE MINING REC-
LAMATION AND ENFORCEMENT

	1982 actual	1983 est.	1984 est.
Executive level V	1	1	1
ES–4	2	2	3
ES–3	3	3	3
ES–1	4	4	3
Subtotal	10	10	10
GS/GM–15	40	40	40
GS/GM–14	77	77	76
GS/GM–13	121	120	120
GS–12	150	150	155
GS–11	91	95	97
GS–9	28	22	20
GS–8	13	13	13
GS–7	59	65	58
GS–6	32	30	28
GS–5	42	40	41
GS–4	52	47	50
GS–3	20	22	23
Subtotal	725	721	721
Total permanent positions	735	731	731
Unfilled positions, end of year	−60	−10	−10
Total permanent employment, end of year	675	721	721

Reprinted from the 1984 *Appendix*, p. II–35.

Part 3: Supplementals and Rescissions

This part is divided into two sections. Section I contains the supplemental appropriations requested by the president for fiscal 1983. Section II contains the proposed rescissions for fiscal 1983. Both sections use the same type of tables as those used in part I of the *Appendix*.

Part 4: Off-Budget Federal Entities

This part contains detailed budgets for certain federal agencies or other activities that by law are not included in the budget and are listed in the *Appendix* for informational purposes only. They include the Board of Governors of the Federal Reserve, Federal Financing Bank, Postal Service, Rural Electrification Administration, Rural Telephone Bank, SPR Petroleum Account, the United States Railway Association, and the United States Synthetic Fuels Corporation. The tables used in this section are the same as those used in part I of the *Appendix*.

Part 5: Other Materials

The material provided in part 5 is required by the Congressional Budget Act of 1974. It includes a list of appropriations with advance funding provisions and appropriations with forward funding provisions. This part also contains a statement of amendments and revisions to fiscal 1983 budget authority requests. These requests were sent to Congress by the president after the 1983 budget was submitted but before the fiscal 1984 budget was submitted.

Part 6: Government-sponsored Enterprises

Government-sponsored enterprises are established and chartered by the federal government and supervised by a federal agency but are privately owned and financed. These budgets are not reviewed by the president and are included in the *Appendix* for informational purposes only. They have been prepared by the enterprises themselves, not by OMB. The enterprises are Banks for cooperatives, Federal Home Loan Bank Board, Federal Home Loan Mortgage Corporation, Federal Intermediate Credit Banks, Federal land banks, Federal National Mortgage Association, and Student Loan Marketing Association. The tables used in this section are the same as those used in part I of the *Appendix*.

CHAPTER 12

MAJOR THEMES AND ADDITIONAL BUDGET DETAILS

Major Themes and Additional Budget Details provides additional explanations and justifications for the major proposals that make up the president's budget. It was included as part of the president's budget for the first time last year. This year *Major Themes* was not submitted to Congress with the budget. It is expected to be published separately in March or April.

Last year, *Major Themes* listed the president's budget proposals by category. Each category began with a narrative explanation of its purposes and goals. The individual proposals making up the category were described by the following elements: program description; proposed change; rationale; and effects of the proposed change.

A table, similar to table 16, was included for each proposal. Note the following points in table 16:

1. The table is in millions of dollars.

TABLE 16

CHILD WELFARE BLOCK GRANT

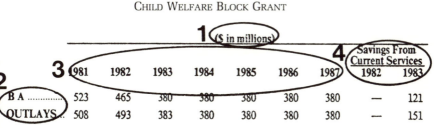

	1981	1982	1983	1984	1985	1986	1987	Savings From Current Services 1982	1983
B A	523	465	380	380	380	380	380	—	121
OUTLAYS ...	508	493	383	380	380	380	380	—	151

Reprinted from Office of Management and Budget, *Major Themes and Additional Budget Details, Fiscal Year 1983* (Washington, D.C.: Government Printing Office, 1982), p. 26.

2. Both budget authority and outlays are included.

3. The figures listed for fiscal 1981 are the actual amounts spent in that year. The figures for fiscal 1982 are the best current estimate for that year. The figures for fiscal 1983 are the administration's proposal. The figures for fiscal 1984–1987 are merely projections of the current proposal to those years, and they will change as the budgets for those years are actually submitted to Congress.

4. These are estimated savings from the current services estimate for fiscal 1983, not the level of spending in fiscal 1982.

Major Themes is a highly partisan presentation that must be carefully used. The information it provides is only a brief statement of the administration's proposals; it is not intended to be a complete description of the pros and cons of each issue.

CHAPTER 13

THE UNITED STATES BUDGET IN BRIEF

The *Budget of the United States Government in Brief* (hereafter referred to as *Budget in Brief*) is a summary of the *Budget of the United States Government* described in chapter 10 of this book. The *Budget in Brief* is the least technical and most concise presentation of the president's budget proposal and is intended for use by the public. All information, including the graphs and tables, is displayed in a more readable manner than in any of the other budget documents.

Because of its apparent simplicity, however, great care must be taken when using the *Budget in Brief*. Its narrative is written in a style that emphasizes the best parts of the president's program. Because of the lack of detailed backup data, however, the *Budget in Brief* does not contain enough information to permit an independent analysis of the administration's claims.

The *Budget in Brief* uses graphs to display much of the information provided in tables in the *Budget*. Figure 2, for example, displays the level of outlays for function 150: International Affairs.

This same information shown in figure 2 is presented more precisely and in greater detail in table 17 from the *Budget*.

The summary tables in the *Budget in Brief* also are similar to those in the *Budget*. They are not exact duplicates, however, and tend to reduce the amount of information presented for ease of reading. In addition, not all summary tables from the *Budget* are included in the *Budget in Brief*.

All other information in the *Budget in Brief* is either self-evident, presented in the same manner, or an exact duplicate of that described in chapter 10 of this book.

FIGURE 2

OUTLAYS FOR INTERNATIONAL AFFAIRS

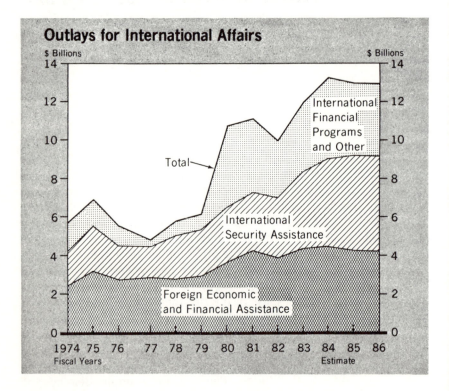

Reprinted from Office of Management and Budget, *The United States Budget in Brief, Fiscal Year 1984* (Washington, D.C.: Government Printing Office, 1983), p. 34.

TABLE 17

NATIONAL NEED: CONDUCTING INTERNATIONAL RELATIONS

(Functional code 150; in millions of dollars)

Major missions and programs	1982 actual	1983 estimate	1984 estimate	1985 estimate	1986 estimate
OUTLAYS					
Foreign aid:					
International security assistance:					
Economic support fund	2,299	2,831	2,944	2,921	2,903
Foreign military sales credit	501	880	1,006	998	1,000
Military assistance	176	242	490	685	772
Other	330	221	270	291	312
Offsetting receipts	−199	−155	−112	−101	−103
Subtotal, international security assistance	3,107	4,019	4,598	4,793	4,884
Foreign economic and financial assistance:					
Multilateral development banks	1,063	1,274	1,407	1,366	1,247
International organizations	238	205	205	193	196
Agency for International Development	1,524	1,715	1,773	1,812	1,848
Public Law 480 food aid	929	1,035	1,052	1,001	975
Peace Corps	103	109	108	109	109
Refugee assistance	382	401	366	340	334
Other	−22	26	41	49	59
Offsetting receipts	−361	−430	−466	−493	−519
Subtotal, foreign economic and financial assistance	3,856	4,335	4,487	4,377	4,248
Total, foreign aid	**6,963**	**8,354**	**9,085**	**9,170**	**9,132**
Conduct of foreign affairs:					
Administration of foreign affairs	1,045	1,145	1,352	1,492	1,541
International organizations and conferences	544	512	602	644	662
Other	41	46	48	48	48
Subtotal, conduct of foreign affairs	1,630	1,704	2,001	2,184	2,250
Foreign information and exchange activities	571	704	828	889	1,052
International financial programs:					
Export-Import Bank	1,173	1,192	1,433	853	566
Special defense acquisition fund	−204	−196	−147	−49	73
Foreign military sales trust fund (net)	188	500	400	300	200
Other	−166	−141	−173	−177	−174
Offsetting receipts	−80	−82	−84	−85	−87
Subtotal, international financial programs	911	1,272	1,430	841	577
Deductions for offsetting receipts	−92	−94	−94	−92	−92
Total, outlays	**9,982**	**11,939**	**13,250**	**12,992**	**12,920**
ADDENDUM					
Off-budget Federal entity:					
Federal Financing Bank:					
Overseas Private Investment Corporation:					
Outlays	−5	−5	−6	−5	−5
Foreign military sales credit:					
Budget authority	2,923	3,538	4,869	4,286	4,425
Outlays	2,288	2,848	4,187	3,495	3,436
Total:					
Budget authority	2,923	3,538	4,869	4,286	4,425
Outlays	2,283	2,843	4,181	3,490	3,431

Reprinted from Office of Management and Budget, *Budget of the United States Government, Fiscal Year 1984* (Washington, D.C.: Government Printing Office, 1983), p. 5–21.

CHAPTER 14

SPECIAL ANALYSES, BUDGET OF THE UNITED STATES GOVERNMENT

Special Analyses, Budget of the United States Government (hereafter referred to as *Special Analyses*) is a series of eleven technical reports on the budget. Some of these are required by the Budget Act. The others are provided to enable readers to evaluate the budget from a number of different perspectives or to emphasize certain parts of the president's program. The analyses cut across all functions and agencies and, for the most part, do not discuss individual line items. The information is presented in a form substantially different from that found in any of the other budget documents.

The eleven analyses can be divided into three categories. Category 1 consists of two alternative views of the budget: (1) *Current Services Estimates,* and (2) *Federal Transactions in the National Income Accounts.* Category 2 consists of seven cross-functional analyses: (1) *Funds in the Budget;* (2) *Investment, Operating, and Other Budget Outlays;* (3) *Borrowing, Debt, and Investment;* (4) *Federal Credit Programs;* (5) *Tax Expenditures;* (6) *Federal Aid to State and Local Governments;* and (7) *Civilian Employment in the Executive Branch.* Category 3 consists of two analyses of the budget that illustrate selected general areas of federal government involvement: (1) *Civil Rights Activities,* and (2) *Research and Development.* The tables used in these reports are usually explained in the analysis where they are found, or they are self-explanatory. This chapter describes each analysis and discusses those tables that require further explanation or emphasis.

CATEGORY ONE: **Alternative Views of the Budget**

Special Analysis A
Current Services Estimates

The current services estimates are required by the Budget Act.[1] Their purpose is to show what the budget authority, outlays, and receipts would be if the federal government were to continue to do in the next budget the exact same things it is doing in this year's budget, or, as the budget states, "if we simply left the federal government on automatic pilot through next year."[2] These estimates are not proposals for new spending or projections as to what spending will be next year. They merely are a device with which to evaluate the president's program, since any proposal that deviates from the current services level for an activity shows an increase or decrease from existing policy.

Current services estimates "reflect the expected costs of continuing ongoing Federal programs at 1983 levels, in real terms, without policy change; that is, they omit all proposed and pending new initiatives, presidential or congressional, that are not now enacted."[3] The specific guidelines used by the president to determine the current services estimates are included in "Current Services Estimates," (pages A-3– A-4).

The following rules are usually applied: (1) The economic assumptions applied are those discussed in the *Budget*.[4] (2) All programs are adjusted for inflation, except those that, by existing law, will not be so increased in fiscal 1984. (3) Entitlement programs that have built-in cost-of-living increases in their benefits are increased to reflect those changes. In addition, entitlements are increased (or decreased) to reflect changes in the number of beneficiaries expected to result from the economic assumptions. (4) Previously enacted changes in programs that are scheduled to become effective in fiscal 1984 are included. Newly proposed or otherwise pending changes are not. (5) Proposed rescissions are not included. Proposed deferrals, however, are assumed to be approved by Congress and are included.[5]

Table 18 and 19 exemplify two major types of tables in the current services analysis. Note the following points in table 18:

1. The table is in billions of dollars.
2. The first column, (1982), shows the actual expenditures in that year. Column 2, (current services, 1983 estimate), shows the estimate of providing in fiscal 1983 what was provided in 1982. Column 3, (current services, 1984 estimate), shows the cost of continuing to provide the same level of service in fiscal 1984. Column 4 shows the administration's actual budget proposal for fiscal 1984. Column 4 compared to column 3 shows what programmatic changes the president is proposing.

TABLE 18

CURRENT SERVICES OUTLAYS BY AGENCY

1 (In billions of dollars)

2	1982 actual	Current services		1984 administration proposals	1984 difference
		1983 estimate	1984 estimate		
Legislative branch	1.4	1.5	1.6	1.6	*
The Judiciary	.7	.8	.9	.9	— *
Executive Office of the President	.1	.1	.1	.1	*
Funds Appropriated to the President	6.1	7.1	7.6	7.9	.3
Department of Agriculture	36.2	45.6	39.1	35.0	— 4.1
Department of Commerce	2.0	2.0	2.0	1.7	— .4
Department of Defense—Military	182.9	208.8	247.0	238.6	— 8.4
Department of Defense—Civil	3.0	2.9	2.7	2.2	— .5
Education	14.1	14.4	14.3	13.5	— .8
Energy	7.6	8.8	9.5	8.8	— .6
Department of Health and Human Services	251.3	276.4	296.6	288.8	— 7.8
Department of Housing and Urban Development	14.5	15.0	15.1	13.7	— 1.3
Department of the Interior	3.9	4.0	3.9	3.6	— .3
Department of Justice	2.6	3.0	3.0	3.3	.3
Department of Labor	30.7	41.2	34.8	34.3	— .5
Department of State	2.2	2.3	2.6	2.6	*
Department of Transportation	19.9	21.1	25.3	24.4	— .9
Department of the Treasury	110.5	117.6	136.2	135.0	— 1.2
Environmental Protection Agency	5.1	4.4	4.1	4.1	— .1
National Aeronautics and Space Administration	6.0	6.7	6.9	7.0	*
Veterans Administration	23.9	24.4	26.0	25.7	— .3
Office of Personnel Management	20.0	21.5	23.6	23.2	— .5
Other independent agencies	13.1	12.5	13.0	11.4	— 1.6
Allowances				1.9	.9	— .9
Undistributed offsetting receipts	— 29.3	— 36.2	— 37.6	— 39.6	— 2.0
Total outlays	**728.4**	**806.1**	**880.3**	**848.5**	**— 31.8**
Memorandum:					
Off-budget outlays	17.3	16.9	17.1	14.0	— 3.0
Total, including off-budget outlays	745.7	823.0	897.3	862.5	— 34.8

*$50 million or less.

Reprinted from Office of Management and Budget, *Special Analyses, Budget of the United States Government, Fiscal Year 1984* (Washington, D.C.: Government Printing Office, 1983), p. A–8.

Note the following points in table 19:

1. The table is in millions of dollars.

2. This is the budget function number.[6]

3. This is the subfunction number.

4. The first column, (1982), is the actual expenditures in that year. Column 2, (current services, 1983 estimate), is the estimate of providing in fiscal 1983 what was provided in 1982. Column 3, (current services, 1984 estimate), is the cost of continuing to provide the same level of service in fiscal year 1984. Column 4 compared to column 3 shows what changes the president is proposing.

The other tables in this analysis provide more detail on the information given in tables 18 and 19.

Special Analysis B
Federal Transactions in the National Income Accounts

The national income accounts (NIA) provide a detailed statistical description of overall economic activity in the United States economy. They depict in dollar terms the composition and use of the nation's output and the distribution of national income to different recipients.

This technical analysis shows the role of federal finances in the NIA. It is divided into three sections: the size, composition, and trends in federal sector receipts and expenditures; quarterly estimates of federal receipts and expenditures; and the major differences between the federal budget and the NIA.

The tables in this analysis are explained fully in the narrative that accompanies them.

CATEGORY TWO: Cross-functional Analyses

Special Analysis C
Funds in the Budget

This report analyzes the budget in terms of its two major funds— federal funds and trust funds. Federal funds are derived mainly from government taxes and borrowing and are used for all of the general purposes of the government. Trust funds are derived from specific taxes and other receipts (such as the Social Security tax) in accordance with the terms of federal law, and such funds can be used only for the specific purpose for which the tax was levied. Separating the two funds as is

TABLE 19

Current Services Budget Authority by Function and Program

(In millions of dollars)

	1982 actual	Current services 1983 estimate	Current services 1984 estimate	1984 administration proposals
407 Other transportation	88	110	114	116
Deductions for offsetting receipts	−116	−87	−85	−85
Total budget authority	21,256	26,676	28,551	27,780
450 COMMUNITY AND REGIONAL DEVELOPMENT				
451 Community development:				
Community development block grants	3,456	3,456	3,677	3,500
Urban development action grants	474	440	468	196
Rental rehabilitation grants (proposed)				150
Urban homesteading		12	12	12
Other programs	361	459	380	368
Proposed legislation				−26
Subtotal, Community development	4,291	4,367	4,538	4,200
452 Area and regional development:				
Rural development	590	777	922	890
Economic development assistance	224	192	238	18
Indian programs	1,156	1,135	1,152	1,080
Regional commissions	159	173	184	
Tennessee Valley Authority	129	176	126	75
Offsetting receipts	−274	−277	−291	−286
Subtotal, Area and regional development	1,984	2,177	2,330	1,777
453 Disaster relief and insurance:				
SBA disaster loans				
Disaster relief	302	130	*	*
National flood insurance fund		71	71	71
Other	62	55	57	57
Subtotal, Disaster relief and insurance	363	256	128	128
Deductions for offsetting receipts	−34	−34	−34	−34
Total budget authority	6,604	6,766	6,962	6,071
500 EDUCATION, TRAINING, EMPLOYMENT, AND SOCIAL SERVICES				
501 Elementary, secondary, and vocational education:				
Education for the disadvantaged	3,041	3,168	3,361	3,014
Special programs and populations	537	534	566	479
Proposed legislation				50
Indian education	343	334	345	250
Impact aid	466	480	511	465
Education for the handicapped	1,069	1,110	1,178	1,110
Vocational and adult education	742	824	873	7
Proposed legislation				493
Other	206	207	218	162
Proposed legislation				−1
Subtotal, Elementary, secondary, and vocational education	6,403	6,658	7,052	6,030

Reprinted from 1984 *Special Analyses*, "Current Services Estimates," p. A–24.

done in this analysis shows the amount of budget authority and outlays available for discretionary activities and those that already are committed to a specific purpose, a comparison that is not possible by looking at the *Budget*, where they are combined. This analysis also shows the balance remaining in each trust fund, its expected outlays in fiscal 1984, and its projected solvency.

Special Analysis D
Investment, Operating, and Other Budget Outlays

This report separates the outlays in the *Budget* into two categories: current and capital expenditures. "Current" or operating expenses are programs that provide benefits primarily in the year in which the spending occurs (e.g., salaries and rents). Investment programs provide future benefits through the acquisition of physical, financial, or other intangible assets (e.g., buildings). For the reasons explained in the analysis, *this should not be considered to be a federal capital budget.*

The tables in this analysis are explained in detail in the narrative that accompanies them.

Special Analysis E
Borrowing, Debt, and Investment

This analysis reviews a variety of issues related to the size and impact of the past, current, and future borrowing needs of the government—the federal debt. It includes discussions on the size and growth of the federal debt, the interest on the federal debt, agency borrowing, the statutory debt limit, government-guaranteed borrowing, and borrowing by government-sponsored enterprises.[7] The tables in this section are either self-explanatory or are explained in the narrative.

Special Analysis F
Federal Credit Programs

This analysis has become more important over the past few years as federal credit programs have become better understood and scrutinized by Congress.

This report analyzes all of the credit programs in the budget: on-budget and off-budget direct loans, federal guarantees of private lending, direct loans by privately owned government-sponsored enterprises, and federal tax-exempt credit.[8] This is different from *Special Analysis E*, which reviews the borrowing done by the federal government itself.

Credit programs are another means by which the government tries to accomplish its goals and are an alternative to federal spending.

A key concept used in this analysis is the "credit budget." The credit budget does not include credit programs in addition to those in the unified budget. It is an alternative presentation designed to correct the problems of placing the credit programs side-by-side with the spending programs.

The major provisions of the credit budget are as follows: (1) All federal credit programs are displayed on a gross basis. The unified budget shows only the net level and obscures the actual amount of new activity. (2) All credit activity is recorded at the point at which the government can exercise some control. For direct loans this is when the federal government enters into a loan obligation, a binding agreement to provide the money. For loan guarantees this is when the federal government makes a firm commitment to pay the lender in the event that the borrower defaults. The unified budget records credit programs only at the point the loans are actually made, or when the federal government pays the borrower. (3) All federal loans and loan guarantees are included, regardless of whether they are made by an on-budget or off-budget agency.

The tables in this analysis are explained fully in the narrative.

Special Analysis G
Tax Expenditures

Tax expenditures are provisions of the tax code that encourage individuals or corporations to do something by granting them a decrease in their taxes. They are the third budgetary means by which the government tries to accomplish its goals and, therefore, are an alternative to federal spending. This analysis estimates the revenue loss attributed to each of the many different tax expenditures that existed as of December 31, 1982.

The primary table in this analysis displays the tax expenditures by function and is self-explanatory.

Special Analysis H
Federal Aid To State and Local Governments

This report describes and analyzes federal support for state and local governments through grants-in-aid and loans. Unlike the earlier analyses, this section is less technical and more rhetorical and attempts to place the president's program in the best light. An independent review of the tables is crucial to a proper understanding of the federal government's role in this area.

Tables 20 and 21 exemplify the two major tables in this section. Note the following points in table 20:

1. Budget authority and outlays are included in the same table.
2. The table is in millions of dollars.
3. Column 3, (1984), is the president's proposal. Column 1, (1982), is the actual level for fiscal 1982. Column 2 is the current estimate of the level of spending that will take place in 1983.

Note the following points in table 21.

1. The table is in millions of dollars.
2. "Net loans" are new direct loans less loan repayments.
3. "Outstandings" are the total direct loans made to date minus loans repaid.
4. Column 3 is the president's proposal. Column 1 is the actual level for fiscal 1982. Column 2 is the current estimate of the level of credit that will be extended in 1983.
5. Direct loan programs are listed separately from guaranteed loan programs.

Special Analysis I
Civilian Employment in the Executive Branch

This analysis is a brief description of the levels of federal civilian employment, both in the aggregate and by agency.

CATEGORY THREE: Selected Areas of Federal Involvement

Special Analysis J
Civil Rights Activities

This analysis describes the various federal statutory, regulatory, and administrative efforts to prohibit discrimination. It discusses the administration's efforts in these areas, mostly in narrative form.

Special Analysis K
Research and Development

The federal government supports research and development activities in thirty-one different agencies. This analysis describes the different activities undertaken, by agency.

TABLE 20

FEDERAL GRANTS TO STATE AND LOCAL GOVERNMENTS, OUTLAYS AND BUDGET AUTHORITY

(In millions of dollars)

Function, agency and program	Functional code [1]	Outlays			Budget Authority		
		1982 actual	1983 estimate	1984 estimate	1982 actual	1983 estimate	1984 estimate
National defense:							
Department of Defense—Military:							
National Guard centers construction	051	29	30	30	29	30	30
Federal Emergency Management Agency	054	39	46	73	80	91	141
Total, national defense	050	68	76	103	109	121	171
Energy:							
Energy Activities: Energy conservation grants	272	346	404	174	129	176	75
Tennessee Valley Authority	271	163	188	193			
Total, energy	270	509	592	368	129	176	75
Natural resources and environment:							
Department of Agriculture:							
Watershed and flood prevention operations	301	144	91	15	140	65	28
Resource conservation and development	302	13	7	7	11	3	5
Forest research	302	10	5	4	10	5	
State and private forestry	302	32	33	2	34	35	
Department of Commerce:							
NOAA—Coastal zone management	302	33	15	11	3	4	
NOAA—Operations research and facilities	306	50	68	12	50	68	12
Department of the Interior:							
Fish and Wildlife Service Grants	303	148	163	168	157	153	171
Operation of the National Park System	303	1	1				
National recreation and preservation	303	1	2		2	2	
Park Construction	303	2	7		8	7	
Urban park and recreation fund	303	31	36				
Land and water conservation fund	303	211		30			

[1] For a description of these codes, see Table 14 in the *Budget of the United States Government, 1984.*

Reprinted from 1984 *Special Analyses,* "Federal Aid to State and Local Governments," p. H–27.

TABLE 21

Credit Assistance to State and Local Governments

1 (In millions of dollars)

Function, agency and program		1982 [a] actual	1983 estimate	1984 estimate
5 Direct Loans				
Natural resources and environment:				
Department of the Interior:				
Bureau of Reclamation loan program	New loans	30	25	40
2	Net loans	24	20	35
	Outstandings	331	351	387
Drought emergency loan fund	New loans			
	Net loans	−6	−3	−3
3	Outstandings	19	16	14
Total, natural resources and environment	New loans	30	25	40
	Net loans	18	17	32
	Outstandings	350	367	401
Agriculture and Commerce and housing credit:				
Department of Agriculture:				
Agriculture credit insurance fund and rural housing insurance funds	New loans	1	1	1
	Net loans	−1	−*	−*
	Outstandings	1	1	1
Transportation:				
Department of Transportation:				
Federal aid highways (trust fund)	New loans	24	8	16
	Net loans	24	8	16
	Outstandings	39	47	62
Right-of-way revolving fund	New loans	1		
	Net loans	1		
	Outstandings	196	196	196
Total, transportation	New loans	25	8	16
	Net loans	25	8	16
	Outstandings	235	243	258
Community and regional development:				
Department of Agriculture:				
Rural development insurance fund	New loans	955	809	675
	Net loans	−89	21	−108
	Outstandings	153	173	65
Department of Commerce:				
Drought assistance program	New loans	*		
	Net loans	4	−4	−4
	Outstandings	94	90	86
Coastal energy impact fund	New loans	29	15	9
	Net loans	28	14	7
	Outstandings	95	108	115
Department of Housing and Urban Development:				
Urban renewal programs	New loans	22	15	8
	Net loans	−11	−1	
	Outstandings	1		
Revolving fund (liquidating programs)	New loans		*	
	Net loans	−20	−21	−22
	Outstandings	442	422	400

* $500 thousand or less.

Reprinted from *Special Analyses*, "Federal Aid to State and Local Governments," p. H–35.

FY 1983—FIRST CONCURRENT RESOLUTION ON THE BUDGET

That the Congress hereby determines and declares that the Second Concurrent Resolution on the Budget for Fiscal Year 1982 is hereby revised, the First Concurrent Resolution on the Budget for Fiscal Year 1983 is hereby established, and the appropriate budgetary levels for Fiscal Years 1984 and 1985 are hereby set forth.

(a) The following budgetary levels are appropriate for the fiscal years beginning on October 1, 1981, October 1, 1982, October 1, 1983, and October 1, 1984:

(1) The recommended levels of Federal revenues are as follows:

Fiscal year 1982: $628,400,000,000.
Fiscal year 1983: $665,900,000,000.
Fiscal year 1984: $738,000,000,000.
Fiscal year 1985: $821,400,000,000.

and the amounts by which the aggregate levels of Federal revenues should be changed are as follows:

Fiscal year 1982: −$200,000,000.
Fiscal year 1983: +$20,900,000,000.

Fiscal year 1984: +$36,000,000,000.
Fiscal year 1985: +$41,400,000,000.

(2) The appropriate levels of total new budget authority are as follows:

Fiscal year 1982: $777,672,000,000.
Fiscal year 1983: $822,390,000,000.
Fiscal year 1984: $878,473,000,000.
Fiscal year 1985: $960,611,000,000.

(3) The appropriate levels of total budget outlays are as follows:

Fiscal year 1982: $734,100,000,000.
Fiscal year 1983: $769,818,000,000.
Fiscal year 1984: $821,928,000,000.
Fiscal year 1985: $881,356,000,000.

(4) The amounts of the deficits in the budget which are ap-

propriate in the light of economic conditions and all other relevant factors are as follows:

    Fiscal year 1982: $105,700,000,000.
    Fiscal year 1983: $103,918,000,000.
    Fiscal year 1984: $83,928,000,000.
    Fiscal year 1985: $59,956,000,000.

    (5) The appropriate levels of the public debt are as follows:
    Fiscal year 1982: $1,143,100,000,000.
    Fiscal year 1983: $1,290,200,000,000.
    Fiscal year 1984: $1,420,219,000,000.
    Fiscal year 1985: $1,533,491,000,000.

and the amounts by which the current temporary statutory limits on such debt should be accordingly increased are as follows:

    Fiscal year 1982: $63,300,000,000.
    Fiscal year 1983: $147,100,000,000.
    Fiscal year 1984: $130,019,000,000.
    Fiscal year 1985: $113,272,000,000.

    (6) The appropriate levels of total Federal credit activity for the fiscal years beginning on October 1, 1981, and October 1, 1982, are as follows:
    Fiscal year 1982:
      (A) New direct loan obligations, $63,600,000,000.
      (B) New primary loan guarantee commitments, $74,900,000,000.
      (C) New secondary loan guarantee commitments, $69,000,000,000.
    Fiscal year 1983:
      (A) New direct loan obligations, $59,700,000,000.
      (B) New primary loan guarantee commitments, $101,900,000,000.
      (B) New secondary loan guarantee commitments, $68,300,000,000.

    (b) The Congress hereby determines and declares the appropriate levels of budget authority, and budget outlays, for the fiscal years 1982 through and inclusive of 1985 and the appropriate levels of new direct loan obligations, new primary loan guarantee commitments, and new secondary loan guarantee commitments for fiscal years 1982 and 1983 for each major functional category are:

    (1) National Defense (050):
    Fiscal year 1982:
      (A) New budget authority, $218,200,000,000.
      (B) Outlays, $187,550,000,000.
      (C) New direct loan obligations, $0.
      (D) New primary loan guarantee commitment, $0.
      (E) New secondary loan guarantee commitments, $0.
    Fiscal year 1983:
      (A) New budget authority, $253,566,000,000.
      (B) Outlays, $213,966,000,000.
      (C) New direct loan obligations, $50,000,000.

(D) New primary loan guarantee commitments, $50,000,000.

(E) New secondary loan guarantee commitments, $0.

Fiscal year 1984:

(A) New budget authority, $279,483,000,000.

(B) Outlays, $243,283,000,000.

Fiscal year 1985:

(A) New budget authority, $323,650,000,000.

(B) Outlays, $279,000,000,000.

(2) International Affairs (150):

Fiscal year 1982:

(A) New budget authority, $16,750,000,000.

(B) Outlays, $11,400,000,000.

(C) New direct loan obligations, $10,400,000,000.

(D) New primary loan guarantee commitments, $8,100,000,000.

(E) New secondary loan guarantee commitments, $0.

Fiscal year 1983:

(A) New budget authority, $15,900,000,000.

(B) Outlays, $11,500,000,000.

(C) New direct loan obligations, $10,200,000,000.

(D) New primary loan guarantee commitments, $9,300,000,000.

(E) New secondary loan guarantee commitments, $0.

Fiscal year 1984:

(A) New budget authority, $16,400,000,000.

(B) Outlays, $11,900,000,000.

Fiscal year 1985:

(A) New budget authority, $21,000,000,000.

(B) Outlays, $11,800,000,000.

(3) General Science, Space, and Technology (250):

Fiscal year 1982:

(A) New budget authority, $7,000,000,000.

(B) Outlays, $7,000,000.

(C) New direct loan obligations, $200,000,000.

(D) New primary loan guarantee commitments, $0.

(E) New secondary loan guarantee commitments, $0.

Fiscal year 1983:

(A) New budget authority, $7,800,000,000.

(B) Outlays, $7,600,000,000.

(C) New direct loan obligations, $200,000,000.

(D) New primary loan guarantee commitments, $0.

(E) New secondary loan guarantee commitments, $0.

Fiscal year 1984:

(A) New budget authority, $7,700,000,000.

(B) Outlays, $7,800,000,000.

Fiscal year 1985:

(A) New budget authority, $7,300,000,000.

(B) Outlays, $7,400,000,000.

(4) Energy (270):
  Fiscal year 1982:
    (A) New budget authority, $4,800,000,000.
    (B) Outlays, $6,400,000,000.
    (C) New direct loan obligations, $10,300,000,000.
    (D) New primary loan guarantee commitments, $400,000,000.
    (E) New secondary loan guarantee commitments, $0.
  Fiscal year 1983:
    (A) New budget authority, $4,800,000,000.
    (B) Outlays, $4,500,000,000.
    (C) New direct loan obligations, $12,000,000,000.
    (D) New primary loan guarantee commitments, $500,000,000.
    (E) New secondary loan guarantee commitments, $0.
  Fiscal year 1984:
    (A) New budget authority, $3,950,000,000
    (B) Outlays, $3,300,000,000.
  Fiscal year 1985:
    (A) New budget authority, $3,800,000,000.
    (B) Outlays, $3,000,000,000.
(5) Natural Resources and Environment (300):
  Fiscal year 1982:
    (A) New budget authority, $10,300,000,000.
    (B) Outlays, $12,800,000,000.
    (C) New direct loan obligations, $30,000,000.
    (D) New primary loan guarantee commitments, $0.
    (E) New secondary loan guarantee commitments, $0.
  Fiscal year 1983:
    (A) New budget authority, $9,500,000,000.
    (B) Outlays, $10,950,000,000.
    (C) New direct loan obligations, $30,000,000.
    (D) New primary loan guarantee commitments, $0.
    (E) New secondary loan guarantee commitments, $0.
  fiscal year 1984:
    (A) New budget authority, $8,700,000,000.
    (B) Outlays, $9,800,000,000.
  Fiscal year 1985:
    (a) New budget authority, $8,300,000,000.
    (B) Outlays, $8,700,000,000.
(6) Agriculture (350):
  Fiscal year 1982:
    (A) New budget authority, $9,900,000,000.
    (B) Outlays, $13,800,000,000.
    (C) New direct loan obligations, $22,600,000,000.
    (D) New primary loan guarantee commitments, $2,700,000,000.
    (E) New secondary loan guarantee commitments, $0.

  Fiscal year 1983:
    (A) New budget authority, $6,692,000,000.
    (B) Outlays, $9,042,000,000.

(C) New direct loan obligations, $18,100,000,000.
(D) New primary loan guarantee commitments, $2,600,000,000.
(E) New secondary loan guarantee commitments, $0.
Fiscal year 1984:
   (A) New budget authority, $8,300,000,000.
   (B) Outlays, $7,600,000,000.
Fiscal year 1985:
   (A) New budget authority, $6,700,000,000.
   (B) Outlays, $7,110,000,000.
(7) Commerce and Housing Credit (370):
Fiscal year 1982:
   (A) New budget authority, $9,480,000,000.
   (B) Outlays, $3,750,000,000.
   (C) New direct loan obligations, $12,050,000,000.
   (D) New primary loan guarantee commitments, $26,200,000,000.
   (E) New secondary loan guarantee commitments, $68,200,000,000.
Fiscal year 1983:
   (A) New budget authority, $7,100,000,000.
   (B) Outlays, $2,837,000,000.
   (C) New direct loan obligations, $12,100,000,000.
   (D) New primary loan guarantee commitments, $41,000,000,000.
   (E) New secondary loan guarantee commitments, $68,200,000,000.
Fiscal year 1984:
   (A) New budget authority, $7,600,000,000.
   (B) Outlays, $2,521,000,000.
Fiscal year 1985:
   (A) New budget authority, $7,223,000,000.
   (B) Outlays, $1,880,000,000.
(8) Transportation (400):
Fiscal year 1982:
   (A) New budget authority, $20,800,000,000.
   (B) Outlays, $21,300,000,000.
   (C) New direct loan obligations, $400,000,000.
   (D) New primary loan guarantee commitments, $750,000,000.
   (E) New secondary loan guarantee commitments, $3,000,000.
Fiscal Year 1983:
   (A) New budget authority, $21,450,000,000.
   (B) Outlays, $19,900,000,000.
   (C) New direct loan obligations, $500,000,000.
   (D) New primary loan guarantee commitments, $800,000,000.
   (E) New secondary loan guarantee commitments, $3,000,000.

Fiscal Year 1984:
    (A) New budget authority, $21,700,000,000.
    (B) Outlays, $19,700,000,000.
Fiscal Year 1985:
    (A) New budget authority, $22,050,000,000.
    (B) Outlays, $19,600,000,000.
(9) Community and Regional Development (450):
Fiscal Year 1982:
    (A) New budget authority, $7,000,000,000.
    (B) Outlays, $8,500,000,000.
    (C) New direct loan obligations, $2,100,000,000.
    (D) New primary loan guarantee commitments, $900,000,000.
    (E) New secondary loan guarantee commitments, $0.
Fiscal Year 1983:
    (A) New budget authority, $6,900,000,000.
    (B) Outlays, $7,700,000,000.
    (C) New direct loan obligations, $2,200,000,000.
    (D) New primary loan guarantee commitments, $600,000,000.
    (E) New secondary loan guarantee commitments, $0.
Fiscal Year 1984:
    (A) New budget authority, $6,900,000,000.
    (B) Outlays, $7,500,000,000.
Fiscal Year 1985:
    (A) New budget authority, $7,100,000,000.
    (B) Outlays, $7,400,000,000.
(10) Education, Training, Employment and Social Services (500):
Fiscal year 1982:
    (A) New budget authority, $25,400,000,000.
    (B) Outlays, $28,100,000,000.
    (C) New direct loan obligations, $1,300,000,000.
    (D) New primary loan guarantee commitments, $6,500,000,000.
    (E) New secondary loan guarantee commitments, $700,000,000.
Fiscal year 1983:
    (A) New budget authority, $26,832,000,000.
    (B) Outlays, $26,205,000,000.
    (C) New direct loan obligations, $800,000,000.
    (D) New primary loan guarantee commitments, $7,200,000,000.
    (E) New secondary loan guarantee commitments, $0.
Fiscal year 1984:
    (A) New budget authority, $26,700,000,000.
    (B) Outlays, $26,900,000,000.
Fiscal year 1985:
    (A) New budget authority, $26,214,000,000.
    (B) Outlays, $26,161,000,000.

(11) Health (550):
Fiscal year 1982:
    (A) New budget authority, $78,500,000,000.
    (B) Outlays, $73,700,000,000.
    (C) New direct loan obligations, $100,000,000.
    (D) New primary loan guarantee commitments, $100,000,000.
    (E) New secondary loan guarantee commitments, $0.
Fiscal year 1983:
    (A) New budget authority, $79,569,000,000.
    (B) Outlays, $77,816,000,000.
    (C) New direct loan obligations, $100,000,000.
    (D) New primary loan guarantee commitments, $100,000,000.
    (E) New secondary loan guarantee commitments, $0.
Fiscal year 1984:
    (A) New budget authority, $91,725,000,000.
    (B) Outlays, $86,249,000,000.
Fiscal year 1985:
    (A) New budget authority, $103,229,000,000.
    (B) Outlays, $98,830,000,000.
(12) Income Security (600):
Fiscal year 1982:
    (A) New budget authority, $256,792,000,000.
    (B) Outlays, $250,300,000,000.
    (C) New direct loan obligations, $2,800,000,000
    (D) New primary loan guarantee commitments, $17,000,000,000.
    (E) New secondary loan guarantee commitments, $0.
Fiscal year 1983:
    (A) New budget authority, $274,797,000,000.
    (B) Outlays, $270,895,000,000.
    (C) New direct loan obligations, $2,000,000,000.
    (D) New primary loan guarantee commitments, $18,700,000,000.
    (E) New secondary loan guarantee commitments, $0.
Fiscal year 1984:
    (A) New budget authority, $291,042,000,000.
    (B) Outlays, $287,531,000,000.
Fiscal year 1985:
    (A) New budget authority, $322,373,000,000.
    (B) Outlays, $308,858,000,000.
(13) Veterans Benefits and Services (700):
Fiscal year 1982:
    (A) New budget authority, $24,800,000,000.
    (B) Outlays, $23,800,000,000.
    (C) New direct loan obligations, $1,000,000,000.
    (D) New primary loan guarantee commitments, $11,900,000,000.
    (E) New secondary loan guarantee commitments, $0.

Fiscal year 1983:
    (A) New budget authority, $24,560,000,000.
    (B) Outlays, $23,823,000,000.
    (C) New direct loan obligations, $1,000,000,000.,
    (D) New primary loan guarantee commitments, $20,900,000,000.
    (E) New secondary loan guarantee commitments, $0.
Fiscal year 1984:
    (A) New budget authority, $25,746,000,000.
    (B) Outlays, $25,017,000,000.

Fiscal year 1985:
    (A) New budget authority, $26,752,000,000.
    (B) Outlays, $26,497,000,000.
(14) Administration of Justice (750):
Fiscal year 1982:
    (A) New budget authority, $4,500,000,000.
    (B) Outlays, $4,600,000,000.
    (C) New direct loan obligations, $0.
    (D) New primary loan guarantee commitments, $0.
    (E) New secondary loan guarantee commitments, $0.
Fiscal year 1983:
    (A) New budget authority, $4,540,000,000.
    (B) Outlays, $4,650,000,000.
    (C) New direct loan obligations, $0.
    (D) New primary loan guarantee commitments, $0.
    (E) New secondary loan guarantee commitments, $0.
Fiscal year 1984:
    (A) New budget authority, $4,500,000,000.
    (B) Outlays, $4,500,000,000.
Fiscal year 1985:
    (A) New budget authority, $4,500,000,000.
    (B) Outlays, $4,500,000,000.
(15) General Government (800):
Fiscal year 1982:
    (A) New budget authority, $5,200,000,000.
    (B) Outlays, $5,000,000,000.
    (C) New direct loan obligations, $100,000,000.
    (D) New primary loan guarantee commitments, $0.
    (E) New secondary loan guarantee commitments, $0.
Fiscal year 1983:
    (A) New budget authority, $4,800,000,000.
    (B) Outlays, $4,650,000,000.
    (C) New direct loan obligations, $50,000,000.
    (D) New primary loan guarantee commitments, $0.
    (E) New secondary loan guarantee commitments, $0.
Fiscal year 1984:
    (A) New budget authority, $4,500,000,000.
    (B) Outlays, $4,450,000,000.
Fiscal year 1985:
    (A) New budget authority, $4,500,000,000.
    (B) Outlays, $4,300,000,000.

(16) General Purpose Fiscal Assistance (850):
    Fiscal year 1982:
        (A) New budget authority, $6,400,000,000.
        (B) Outlays, $6,300,000,000.
        (C) New direct loan obligations, $200,000,000.
        (D) New primary loan guarantee commitments, $300,000,000.
        (E) New secondary loan guarantee commitments, $0.
    Fiscal year 1983:
        (A) New budget authority, $6,500,000,000.
        (B) Outlays, $6,500,000,000.
        (C) New direct loan obligations, $200,000,000.

        (D) New primary loan guarantee commitments, $0.
        (E) New secondary loan guarantee commitments, $0.
    Fiscal year 1984:
        (A) New budget authority, $6,700,000,000.
        (B) Outlays, $6,700,000,000.
    Fiscal year 1985:
        (A) New budget authority, $6,850,000,000.
        (B) Outlays, $6,850,000,000.
(17) Interest (900):
    Fiscal year 1982:
        (A) New budget authority, $100,700,000,000.
        (B) Outlays, $100,700,000,000.
        (C) New direct loan obligations, $0.
        (D) New primary loan guarantee commitments, $0.
        (E) New secondary loan guarantee commitments, $0.
    Fiscal year 1983:
        (A) New budget authority, $113,200,000,000.
        (B) Outlays, $113,200,000,000.
        (C) New direct loan obligations, $0.
        (D) New primary loan guarantee commitments, $0.
        (E) New secondary loan guarantee commitments, $0.
    Fiscal year 1984:
        (A) New budget authority, $118,000,000,000.
        (B) Outlays, $118,000,000,000.
    Fiscal year 1985:
        (A) New budget authority, $111,500,000,000.
        (B) Outlays, $111,500,000,000.
(18) Allowances (920):
    Fiscal year 1982:
        (A) New budget authority, $2,850,000,000.
        (B) Outlays, $800,000,000.
        (C) New direct loan obligations, $0.
        (D) New primary loan guarantee commitments, $0.
        (E) New secondary loan guarantee commitments, $0.
    Fiscal year 1983:
        (A) New budget authority, −$3,016,000,000.
        (B) Outlays, −$2,816,000,000.
        (C) New direct loan obligations, $0.

      (D) New primary loan guarantee commitments, $0.
      (E) New secondary loan guarantee commitments, $0.
   Fiscal year 1984:
      (A) New budget authority, −$2,383,000,000.
      (B) Outlays, −$2,033,000,000.
   Fiscal year 1985:
      (A) New budget authority, −$2,150,000,000.
      (B) Outlays, −$1,750,000,000.
  (19) Undistributed Offsetting Receipts (950):
   Fiscal year 1982:
      (A) New budget authority, −$31,700,000,000.
      (B) Outlays, −$31,700,000,000.
      (C) New direct loan obligations, $0.
      (D) New primary loan guarantee commitments, $0.
      (E) New secondary loan guarantee commitments, $0.
   Fiscal year 1983:
      (A) New budget authority, −$43,100,000,000.
      (B) New Outlays, −$43,100,000,000.
      (C) New direct loan obligations, $0.
      (D) New primary loan guarantee commitments, $0.
      (E) New secondary loan guarantee commitments, $0.
   Fiscal year 1984:
      (A) New budget authority, −$48,790,000,000.
      (B) Outlays, −$48,790,000,000.
   Fiscal year 1985:
      (A) New budget authority, −$50,280,000,000.
      (B) Outlays −$50,280,000,000.

RECONCILIATION

   SEC. 2. *(a) Not later than July 20, 1982, the Senate committees named in subsection (b) (1) through (7) of this section shall submit their recommendations to the Senate Committee on the Budget and not later than August 1, 1982, the House committees named in subsection (c) (1) through (10) of this section shall submit their recommendations to the House Committee on the Budget. Those recommendations shall be sufficient to accomplish the reductions required by subsections (b) and (c) of this section. After receiving those recommendations, the Committees on the Budget shall report to the House and Senate a reconciliation bill or resolution or both carrying out all such recommendations without any substantive revision.*

SENATE COMMITTEES

   (b)(1) The Senate Committee on Agriculture, Nutrition, and Forestry shall report changes in laws within the jurisdiction of that committee, (A) to require reductions in appropriations for programs authorized by that committee so as to achieve savings in budget authority and outlays, or (B) which provide spending authority as defined in section 401(c)(2)(C) of Public Law 93-344, sufficient to reduce budget authority and outlays, or (C) any combination thereof,

as follows: $779,000,000 in budget authority and $779,000,000 in outlays in fiscal year 1983; $1,083,000,000 in budget authority and $1,083,000,000 in outlays in fiscal year 1984; and $1,428,000,000 in budget authority and $1,428,000,000 in outlays in fiscal year 1985.

(2) The Senate Committee on Armed Services shall report changes in laws within the jurisdiction of that committee which provide spending authority as defined in section 401(c)(2)(C) of Public Law 93-344, sufficient to reduce budget authority by $213,000,000 and outlays by $213,000,000 in fiscal year 1983; to reduce budget authority by $693,000,000 and outlays by $693,000,000 in fiscal year 1984; and to reduce budget authority by $1,231,00,000 and outlays by $1,231,000,000 in fiscal year 1985.

(3) The Senate Committee on Banking, Housing and Urban Affairs shall report changes in laws within the jurisdiction of that committee which provide spending authority as defined in section 401(c)(2)(C) of Public Law 93-344, sufficient to reduce budget authority by $0 and outlays by $695,000,000 in fiscal year 1983; to reduce budget authority by $0 and outlays by $697,000,000 in fiscal year 1984; and to reduce budget authority by $0 and outlays by $687,000,000 in fiscal year 1985.

(4) The Senate Committee on Commerce, Science, and Transportation shall report changes in laws within the jurisdiction of that committee which provide spending authority as defined in section 401(c)(2)(C) of Public Law 93-344, sufficient to reduce budget authority by $4,000,000 and outlays by $4,000,000 in fiscal year 1983; to reduce budget authority by $15,000,000 and outlays by $15,000,000 in fiscal year 1984; and to reduce budget authority by $27,000,000 and outlays by $27,000,000 in fiscal year 1985.

(5) The Senate Committee on Foreign Relations shall report changes in laws within the jurisdiction of that committee which provide spending authority as defined in section 401(c)(2)(C) of Public Law 93-344, sufficient to reduce budget authority by $0 and outlays by $2,000,000 in fiscal year 1983; to reduce budget authority by $2,000,000 and outlays by $8,000,000 in fiscal year 1984; and to reduce budget authority by $4,000,000 and outlays by $15,000,000 in fiscal year 1985.

(6) The Senate Committee on Governmental Affairs shall report changes in laws within the jurisdiction of that committee which provide spending authority as defined in section 401(c)(2)(C) of Public Law 93-344, sufficient to reduce budget authority by $0 and outlays by $374,000,000 in fiscal year 1983; to reduce budget authority by $240,000,000 and outlays by $1,053,000,000 in fiscal year 1984; and to reduce budget authority by $534,000,000 and outlays by $1,793,000,000 in fiscal year 1985.

(7) The Senate Committee on Veterans' Affairs shall report changes in laws within the jurisdiction of that committee which provide spending authority as defined in section 401(c)(2)(C) of Public Law 93-344, sufficient to reduce budget authority by $77,000,000 and outlays by $77,000,000 in fiscal year 1983; to reduce budget authority by $155,000,000 and outlays by $155,000,000 in fiscal year 1984; and to reduce budget authority by $155,000,000 and outlays by $155,000,000 in fiscal year 1985.

HOUSE COMMITTEES

(c)(1) The Committee on Agriculture shall report changes in laws within the jurisdiction of that committee, (A) to require reductions in appropriations for programs authorized by that committee so as to achieve savings in budget authority and outlays, or (B) which provide spending authority as defined in section 401(c)(2)(C) of Public Law 93-344, sufficient to reduce budget authority and outlays, or (C) any combination thereof, as follows: $779,000,000 in budget authority and $779,000,000 in outlays in fiscal year 1983; $1,083,000,000 in budget authority and $1,083,000,000 in outlays in fiscal year 1984; and $1,428,000,000 in budget authority and $1,428,000,000 in outlays in fiscal year 1985.

(2) The House Committee on Armed Services shall report changes in laws within the jurisdiction of that committee which provide spending authority as defined in section 401(c)(2)(C) of Public Law 93-344, sufficient to reduce budget authority by $213,000,000 and outlays by $213,000,000 in fiscal year 1983; to reduce budget authority by $693,000,000 and outlays by $693,000,000 in fiscal year 1984; and to reduce budget authority by $1,231,000,000 and outlays by $1,231,000,000 in fiscal year 1985.

(3) The House Committee on Banking, Finance, and Urban Affairs shall report changes in laws within the jurisdiction of that committee which provide spending authority as defined in section 401(c)(2)(C) of Public Law 93-344, sufficient to reduce budget authority by $0 and outlays by $695,000,000 in fiscal year 1983; to reduce budget authority by $0 and outlays by $697,000,000 in fiscal year 1984; and to reduce budget authority by $0 and outlays by $687,000,000 in fiscal year 1985.

(4) The House Committee on Energy and Commerce shall report changes in laws within the jurisdiction of that committee which provide spending authority as defined in section 401(c)(2)(C) of Public Law 93-344, sufficient to reduce budget authority by $514,000,000 and outlays by $675,000,000 in fiscal year 1983; to reduce budget authority by $741,000,000 and outlays by $739,000,000 in fiscal year 1984; and to reduce budget authority by $815,000,000 and outlays by $811,000,000 in fiscal year 1985.

(5) The House Committee on Foreign Affairs shall report changes in laws within the jurisdiction of that committee which provide spending authority as defined in section 401(c)(2)(C) of Public Law 93-344, sufficient to reduce budget authority by $0 and outlays by $2,000,000 in fiscal year 1983; to reduce budget authority by $2,000,000 and outlays by $8,000,000 in fiscal year 1984; and to reduce budget authority by $4,000,000 and outlays by $15,000,000 in fiscal year 1985.

(6) The House Committee on Merchant Marine and Fisheries shall report changes in laws within the jurisdiction of that committee which provide spending authority as defined in section 401(c)(2)(C) of Public Law 93-344, sufficient to reduce budget authority by $4,000,000 and outlays by $4,000,000 in fiscal year 1983; to reduce budget authority by $15,000,000 and outlays by $15,000,000 in fiscal

year 1984; and to reduce budget authority by $27,000,000 and out-lays by $27,000,000 in fiscal year 1985.

(7) The House Committee on Post Office and Civil Service shall report changes in laws within the jurisdiction of that committee which provide spending authority as defined in section 401(c)(2)(C) of Public Law 93–344, sufficient to reduce budget authority by $0 and outlays by $376,000,000 in fiscal year 1983; to reduce budget authority by $242,000,000 and outlays by $1,061,000,000 in fiscal year 1984; and to reduce budget authority by $538,000,000 and outlays by $1,808,000,000 in fiscal year 1985.

(8) The House Committee on Veterans' Affairs shall report changes in laws within the jurisdiction of that committee which provide spending authority as defined in section 401(c)(2)(C) of Public Law 93–344, sufficient to reduce budget authority by $77,000,000 and outlays by $77,000,000 in fiscal year 1983; to reduce budget authority by $155,000,000 and outlays by $155,000,000 in fiscal year 1984; and to reduce budget authority by $155,000,000 and outlays by $155,000,000 in fiscal year 1985.

(9) The House Committee on Ways and Means shall report changes in laws within the jurisdiction of that committee which provide spending authority as defined in section 401(c)(2)(C) of Public Law 93–344, sufficient to reduce budget authority by $593,000,000 and outlays by $3,755,000,000 in fiscal year 1983; to reduce budget authority by $705,000,000 and outlays by $4,827,000,000 in fiscal year 1984; and to reduce budget authority by $928,000,000 and outlays by $5,168,000,000 in fiscal year 1985.

(10)(A) The House Committee on Ways and Means shall report changes in laws within the jurisdiction of the committee sufficient to increase revenue by $20,900,000,000 for fiscal year 1983; further, the Congress finds that the prospect of unacceptably high deficits in future years requires additional revenues of $36,000,000,000 for fiscal year 1984, and $41,400,000,000 for fiscal year 1985.

(B) If the changes in laws reported to the House Committee on the Budget by the House Committee on Ways and Means pursuant to subsection (a) contain changes involving the imposition of new or expanded taxes to directly finance programs within the jurisdiction of any other committee of the House (including, but not limited to, inland waterways or deep draft ports) or the imposition of any new or expanded user fees within the jurisdiction of any other committee of the House, an appropriate referral pursuant to rule X of the rules of the House should be considered.

SENATE FINANCE COMMITTEE

(d)(1) The Senate Committee on Finance shall report changes in laws within the jurisdiction of that committee which provide spending authority as defined in section 401(c)(2)(C) of Public Law 93–344, sufficient to reduce budget authority by $1,106,000,000 and outlays by $4,429,000,000 in fiscal year 1983; to reduce budget authority by $1,444,000,000 and outlays by $5,564,000,000 in fiscal year 1984; and to reduce budget authority by $1,740,000,000 and outlays by $5,976,000,000 in fiscal year 1985.

(2) The Senate Committee on Finance shall also report changes in laws within the jurisdiction of that committee sufficient to increase revenues as follows: $20,900,000,000 in fiscal year 1983; $36,000,000,000 in fiscal year 1984; and $41,400,000,000 in fiscal year 1985.

(3) The legislation required in paragraphs (1) and (2) of this subsection shall be reported to the Senate no later than July 12, 1982.

MISCELLANEOUS PROVISIONS

SEC. 3. *It shall not be in order in the House or the Senate during fiscal years 1982 and 1983 to consider any bill, resolution, or amendment, except proposed legislation reported in response to reconciliation instructions contained in this resolution, authorizing new direct loan obligations or new loan guarantee commitments unless that bill, resolution, or amendment also provides that the authority to make or guarantee such loans shall be effective only to such extent or in such amounts as are contained in appropriation Acts. This section shall not be applicable to agricultural price support and related programs of the type in operation on January 1, 1982, that are funded through the Commodity Credit Corporation, loans and loan guarantee programs administered by the Veterans' Administration, or bills or resolutions reported to the House or Senate prior to the adoption of this resolution.*

SEC. 4. *(a) No bill or resolution providing new budget authority for fiscal year 1983, or new spending authority described in section 401(c)(2)(C) of the Congressional Budget Act first effective in fiscal year 1983, which exceeds in either the House of Representatives or the Senate, the appropriate allocation or subdivision of such new discretionary budget authority, new budget authority, or new spending authority made pursuant to section 302 of such Act shall be enrolled until after the Congress has completed action on the Second Concurrent Resolution on the Budget required to be reported under section 310 of such Act.*

(b) If Congress increases revenues in a trust fund exempt under section 401(d)(1)(B) of the Congressional Budget Act, 90 percent or more of the receipts of which consist of or will consist of amounts (transferred from the general fund of the Treasury) equivalent to amounts of taxes (related to the purposes for which such outlays are or will be made) received in the Treasury under specified provisions of the Internal Revenue Code of 1954, then for purposes of this section in the House of Representatives, "new discretionary budget authority" and "new spending authority", and for purposes of this section in the Senate, "new budget authority" and "new spending authority" shall not include spending authority or budget authority derived from such trust fund. This subsection shall only apply to trust funds—

(1) exempt under section 401(a)(1)(B) of the Congressional Budget Act,

(2) for which revenues are increased, and

(3) to the extent that such increased revenues exceed the appropriate allocation or subdivision of such new discretionary

budget authority, new budget authority, or new spending authority made pursuant to section 302 of such Act.

SEC. 5. *It is the sense of the Congress that if Congress acts to restore fiscal responsibility and reduces projected budget deficits in a substantial and permanent way, then the Federal Reserve Open Market Committee shall reevaluate its monetary targets in order to assure that they are fully complementary to a new and more restrained fiscal policy.*

SEC. 6. *It is the sense of the Congress that concurrent resolutions on the budget should reflect the full range of fiscal activities of the Federal Government. It is further the sense of the Congress, therefore, that each concurrent resolution on the budget, beginning with the first concurrent resolution on the budget for fiscal year 1984, shall list, for each functional category, the off-budget activities associated with that category, as well as the new budget authority, outlays, new direct loan obligations, new primary loan guarantee commitments, and new secondary loan guarantee commitments associated with that category.*

SEC. 7. *If Congress has not completed action by October 1, 1982, on the Concurrent Resolution on the Budget required to be reported under section 310(a) of the Budget Act for the 1983 fiscal year, then, for purposes of section 311 of such Act, and section 4 of this resolution, this concurrent resolution shall be deemed to be the concurrent resolution required to be reported under section 310(a) of such Act.*

SEC. 8. *It shall not be in order in either the House of Representatives or the Senate to consider any bill or resolution, or amendment thereto, providing—*

(1) new budget authority for fiscal year 1983; or

(2) new spending authority described in section 401(c)(2)(C) of the Budget Act first effective in fiscal year 1983;

within the jurisdiction of any of its committees unless and until such committee makes the allocations or subdivisions required by section 302(b) of the Budget Act, in connection with the most recently agreed to concurrent resolution on the budget.

SEC. 9. *(a) After the Congress has completed action on the concurrent resolution on the budget required to be reported under section 310(a) for fiscal year 1983, and, if a reconciliation bill or resolution, or both, for such fiscal year are required to be reported under section 310(c), after that bill has been enacted into law or that resolution has been agreed to, it shall not be in order in either the House of Representatives or the Senate to consider any bill, resolution, or amendment providing authority for—*

(1) new direct loan obligations for fiscal year 1983:

(2) new primary loan guarantee commitments for fiscal year 1983; or

(3) new secondary loan guarantee commitments for fiscal year 1983;

or any conference report on any such bill or resolution, if—

(A) the enactment of such bill or resolution as reported;

(B) the adoption and enactment of such amendment; or

(C) the enactment of such bill or resolution in the form recommended in such conference report;
would cause the appropriate level of total new direct loan obligations for fiscal year 1983, total new primary loan guarantee commitments for such fiscal year, or total new secondary loan guarantee commitments for such fiscal year set forth in such concurrent resolution on the budget to be exceeded.

(b)(1) The joint explanatory statement accompanying the conference repor: *on this resolution shall include an estimated allocation, based upo*ⁿ *the first section of this resolution as recommended in such conference report, of the appropriate levels of total new direct loan obligations, new primary loan guarantee commitments, and new secondary loan guarantee commitments authority among each committee of the House of Representatives and the Senate which has jurisdiction over bills and resolutions providing such new authority.*

(2) As soon as practicable after this resolution is agreed to every committee of each House, after consulting with the committee or committees of the other House to which all or part of the allocation has been made, subdivide among its subcommittees the allocation of new direct loan obligations, new primary loan guarantee commitments, and new secondary loan guarantee commitments allocated to it in the joint explanatory statement accompanying the conference report on this resolution.

(c) This section shall not be applicable to agricultural price support and related programs of the type in operation on January 1, 1982, that are funded through the Commodity Credit Corporation.

SEC. 10. *It is the sense of Congress that reductions in Federal employment should be accomplished through attrition.*

MARCH 15 REPORTS OF HOUSE ARMED SERVICES AND FOREIGN AFFAIRS COMMITTEES

CHARLES E. TERGITT, FLA.
DANIEL B. STRATTON, N.Y.
RICHARD C. WHITE, TEX.
BILL NICHOLS, ALA.
JACK BRINKLEY, GA.
ROBERT H. MOLLOHAN, W.VA.
DAN DANIEL, VA.
G. V. (SONNY) MONTGOMERY, MISS.
LES ASPIN, WIS.
RONALD V. DELLUMS, CALIF.
PATRICIA SCHROEDER, COLO.
ABRAHAM KAZEN, JR., TEX.
ANTONIO B. WON PAT, GUAM
LARRY MCDONALD, GA.
BOB STUMP, ARIZ.
BEVERLY B. BYRON, MD.
NICHOLAS MAVROULES, MASS.
EARL HUTTO, FLA.
IKE SKELTON, MO.
MARVIN LEATH, TEX.
DAVE MCCURDY, OKLA.
THOMAS M. FOGLIETTA, PA.
ROY DYSON, MD.
DENNIS M. HERTEL, MICH.
JOSEPH F. SMITH, PA.

U.S. House of Representatives

COMMITTEE ON ARMED SERVICES

Washington, D.C. 20515

NINETY-SEVENTH CONGRESS

MELVIN PRICE (ILL.), CHAIRMAN

March 12, 1982

WILLIAM L. DICKINSON, ALA.
G. WILLIAM WHITEHURST, VA.
FLOYD SPENCE, S.C.
ROBIN BEARD, TENN.
DONALD J. MITCHELL, N.Y.
MARJORIE S. HOLT, MD.
ROBERT W. DANIEL, JR., VA.
ELWOOD HILLIS, IND.
DAVID F. EMERY, MAINE
PAUL TRIBLE, VA.
ROBERT E. BADHAM, CALIF.
CHARLES F. DOUGHERTY, PA.
JIM COURTER, N.J.
LARRY J. HOPKINS, KY.
ROBERT W. DAVIS, MICH.
KEN KRAMER, COLO.
DUNCAN L. HUNTER, CALIF.
JAMES L. HILLMAN, PA.
THOMAS F. HARTNETT, S.C.

JOHN J. FORD, CHIEF COUNSEL

Honorable James R. Jones
Chairman
Committee on the Budget
U.S. House of Representatives
Washington, D.C.   20515

Dear Mr. Chairman:

This letter is to convey, in accordance with section 301(c) of the Congressional Budget Act of 1974, the views and estimates of the Committee on Armed Services for budget authority for the National Defense Function (Function 050).

The total request for the National Defense Function is $263.0 billion in budget authority and $221.1 billion in outlays. The total budget authority is composed of $257.5 billion in budget authority ($258.0 billion in total obligational authority) for the Department of Defense and $5.5 billion for programs outside the Department of Defense. These include $5.5 billion for defense nuclear programs administered through the Department of Energy; amounts for civil defense, which is administered by the Federal Emergency Management Agency; funding for the Selective Service System; and a net reduction of $472 million as a result of sales that exceed purchases from the national strategic stockpile.

Due to deficiencies in the material available, the committee was unable to comply with your request to utilize the "CBO current policy baseline" in the preparation of this report. The materials available to the committee provided no meaningful basis for relating the CBO current policy baseline to the President's budget request.

As a result of the submission of the budget on February 8, more than two weeks later than usual, and delays in the submission of more detailed information on the proposed budget that is used by the committee, the committee can offer only general views and estimates at this time.

In general, without making a judgment at this time on specific programs, the committee believes that the level of funding requested for the National Defense Function is justified in terms of the potential threats facing the United States and the improvement in capability in areas of past neglect required by our Armed Forces. However, the committee is mindful that the budget is being examined under extraordinary economic conditions. In the committee's continuing review, as more detailed information is received, a

more refined estimate will be produced and some reductions may be possible. The committee at the very least expects that offsetting reductions can be made in those instances where savings forecast in the President's budget do not materialize.

The committee would point out that very large and disruptive changes in the authorization for defense programs would be required to make significant reductions in defense outlays in fiscal year 1983 and that such reductions could amount to only a small fraction of the projected deficit. More than $70 billion of the estimated $221 billion in outlays for the defense function are estimated to result from appropriations enacted in prior years. An additional $16.6 billion is for military retired pay. Of the remaining $134.4 billion that might be categorized as "relatively controllable under current law," approximately $74 billion is for pay and allowances of civilian and military personnel and approximately $32 billion is for operations and maintenance directly related to readiness. In the remaining areas, procurement, research and development, and military construction, each dollar of outlay reduction can be achieved only with a manyfold larger reduction in budget authority.

For example, to reduce outlays by $1 billion, a reduction of nearly $10 billion would be necessary in the procurement accounts.

The committee would like to bring to your attention certain considerations that will have an impact on the budget authority requirements. The administration's request is based on certain assumptions that, if they fail to materialize, would require either some reduction in the programs to be supported or additional funding beyond what is presently requested.

The Administration's request includes estimates for inflation for fiscal year 1983 and beyond that are somewhat lower than the estimates of the Congressional Budget Office. The committee hopes that inflation will subside at the rate and to the degree that the Administration predicts. However, should the Administration estimates prove low, fact of life increases or program reductions would be required.

The Administration request includes a variety of actions to effect cost savings estimated at more than $7 billion. Many of the these savings are attributed to use of more economic procurement rates and are in line with recommendations made in the past by the Congress and the General Accounting Office. Additional savings proposed in the budget are based on the assumption of legislative action. For example, there is an estimated savings of $89 million from legislation that would modify the cost-of-living adjustment for military retirees by, among other changes, limiting the increase for past retirees whose retired pay is currently larger than the retired pay of members of the same grade and years of service who retired more recently.

Additionally, the Administration has proposed a net savings of $472 million from stockpile purchases and sales. The Administration request includes new purchases of approximately $120 million and receipts of nearly $600 million by sales from the stockpile.

Approximately $402 million of the anticipated receipts, estimated in the budget to be derived from the sale of silver, will require congressional approval before it can be realized.

Since legislation to authorize the sale of silver was enacted as a part of the Omnibus Reconciliation Act of 1981, a subsequent act (P.L. 97-114) restricts the sale of silver until the President redetermines that the silver authorized for disposal is excess to the requirements of the stockpile and the Congress approves of the President's recommended method of disposal. The committee believes that the sale of silver is not in the national interest and recommends that receipts from the sale of silver not be included in the First Concurrent Resolution on the Budget. Further, the Congress has not approved the sale of silver in the past when the issue has been specifically addressed and it is not likely to do so in the future.

The defense budget as submitted by the Administration includes $137 million for legislative contingencies. This amount appears low.

In addition to legislation included in the President's budget, the committee is actively considering educational benefits legislation (G.I. Bill) and is reviewing alternative funding mechanisms that could result in a requirement for fiscal year 1983 budget authority.

You asked that the committee address proposals for spending reductions that will arise from whatever source. The committee believes that the maintenance of adequate national security requires continuing real growth in the budget for national defense. The committee will continue to review specific proposals for spending reductions and, to the extent that they have merit, will incorporate them in authorizing legislation for fiscal year 1983 and subsequent years. However, the committee does not expect that this will significantly change the requirement for growth in the defense budget as proposed by the President for fiscal year 1983 and subsequent years.

In essence, the $263 billion requested by the Administration for the National Defense Function for fiscal year 1983 appears to be the upper limit of the amount required. The committee's more detailed examination should determine if some net reduction may be made. In any event, the committee expects that offsetting adjustments can be made in those instances where new or expanded programs are authorized or where savings proposed in the President's budget are not implemented. The committee would emphasize that only a small portion of the National Defense Function is an entitlement or within the direct spending jurisdiction of the committee and that it does not anticipate that substantial reductions are possible in these areas.

Sincerely,

Melvin Price
Chairman

CLEMENT J. ZABLOCKI, WIS., CHAIRMAN

L. H. FOUNTAIN, N.C.   WILLIAM S. BROOMFIELD, MICH.
DANTE B. FASCELL, FLA.   EDWARD J. DERWINSKI, ILL.
BENJAMIN S. ROSENTHAL, N.Y.   PAUL FINDLEY, ILL.
LEE H. HAMILTON, IND.   LARRY WINN, JR., KANS.
JONATHAN B. BINGHAM, N.Y.   BENJAMIN A. GILMAN, N.Y.
GUS YATRON, PA.   ROBERT J. LAGOMARSINO, CALIF.
STEPHEN J. SOLARZ, N.Y.   WILLIAM F. GOODLING, PA.
DON BONKER, WASH.   JOEL PRITCHARD, WASH.
GERRY E. STUDDS, MASS.   MILLICENT FENWICK, N.J.
ANDY IRELAND, FLA.   ROBERT K. DORNAN, CALIF.
DAN MICA, FLA.   JIM LEACH, IOWA
MICHAEL D. BARNES, MD.   ARLEN ERDAHL, MINN.
HOWARD WOLPE, MICH.   TOBY ROTH, WIS.
GEO. W. CROCKETT, JR., MICH.   OLYMPIA J. SNOWE, MAINE
BOB SHAMANSKY, OHIO   JOHN LE BOUTILLIER, N.Y.
SAM GEJDENSON, CONN.   HENRY J. HYDE, ILL.
MERVYN M. DYMALLY, CALIF.
DENNIS E. ECKART, OHIO
TOM LANTOS, CALIF.
DAVID R. BOWEN, MISS.

JOHN J. BRADY, JR.
CHIEF OF STAFF

𝕮𝖔𝖓𝖌𝖗𝖊𝖘𝖘 𝖔𝖋 𝖙𝖍𝖊 𝖀𝖓𝖎𝖙𝖊𝖉 𝖘𝖙𝖆𝖙𝖊𝖘

𝕮𝖔𝖒𝖒𝖎𝖙𝖙𝖊𝖊 𝖔𝖓 𝕱𝖔𝖗𝖊𝖎𝖌𝖓 𝕬𝖋𝖋𝖆𝖎𝖗𝖘

𝕳𝖔𝖚𝖘𝖊 𝖔𝖋 𝕽𝖊𝖕𝖗𝖊𝖘𝖊𝖓𝖙𝖆𝖙𝖎𝖛𝖊𝖘

𝖂𝖆𝖘𝖍𝖎𝖓𝖌𝖙𝖔𝖓, 𝕯.𝕮.   20515

March 15, 1982

The Honorable James R. Jones
Chairman
Committee on the Budget
A214, HOB Annex 1
U.S. House of Representatives
Washington, D.C.   20515

Dear Mr. Chairman:

By direction of the Committee on Foreign Affairs, I submit herewith
the Views and Estimates Report required by Section 301(c) of the Congressional Budget Act of 1974 in connection with the First Concurrent Resolution on the Budget for Fiscal Year 1983.

The report, which follows, was considered by the Committee in open
session on March 11th, and approved by voice vote.

1. Programs Under the Committee's Authorization Jurisdiction

The President's FY 1983 Budget Request for programs under the
Committee's authorization jurisdiction totals $11.1 billion in budget
authority and $10.1 billion in outlays.

During the First Session, Congress passed legislation authorizing
$6.038 billion in foreign economic and military assistance for FY 1983.
In addition, legislation authorizing $2.85 billion in FY 1983 for the
Department of State, the International Communication Agency (ICA), the
Board for International Broadcasting (BIB), and the Arms Control and
Disarmament Agency (ACDA) is at the House-Senate conference stage. Thus,
Congress has already approved, or is close to approving, $8.8 billion
in FY 1983 authorizations for foreign assistance (excluding Food-for-
Peace and the multilateral development banks), conduct of foreign affairs,
and foreign information and exchange activities, leaving $1.45 billion
of the President's request requiring additional authorization. An
FY 1982 supplemental authorization for Economic Support Funds (ESF) has
also been requested for the Caribbean Basin countries by the President.

At the time of the Committee's consideration of this report, specific
detailed legislative requests for the President's additional budget estimates
had not been submitted by the Administration. Therefore, the Committee
cannot recommend precisely how much of the President's additional authorization requests should be reflected in the First Concurrent Resolution
on the Budget in terms of budget authority and outlays. The Committee can,
however, advise the Budget Committee that the enacted FY 1983 foreign
military and economic assistance authorizations ($6.038 billion) and the
pending State Department, ICA, BIB, and ACDA conference levels ($2.85
billion) will serve as an irreducible base from which the President's
additional $1.45 billion authorization request will be actively considered.

Specifically, the Committee expects to act upon the President's FY
1982-83 economic assistance requests for the Caribbean area and his additional security assistance requests. The Committee also expects to approve
full funding of the FY 1983 requests for State Department and ICA operations.

2. Food-for-Peace (P.L. 480) Levels

   The President's FY 1983 estimate for P.L. 480 budget authority is
$1.028 billion. This includes $650 million for the Title II humanitarian
grant programs distributed by PVOs and the World Food Program. This is
$60 million under the level required by law for Title II unless waived
by the President. The President has not made such a waiver. The Committee
has strongly urged and sponsored Title II minimums in the past, and
therefore recommends that the budget resolution accommodate the full
amount for Title II as mandated by law.

   On a related matter, the Committee also reaffirms its support for the
Agricultural Export Credit Revolving Fund as authorized in Section 1210 of
the Agriculture and Food Act of 1981 and for the funding of that measure
in fiscal year 1983, as expressed in the Statement of Managers on that
legislation, to promote U.S. agricultural exports and thereby benefit
the U.S. economy. While the Fund does not appear to come within the
150 function, the Committee believes $500 million would be an appropriate
one-time financing to place the Fund in operation.

3. Permanent Budget Authorizations Under Committee Jurisdiction

   The Committee has primary jurisdiction over various budget accounts
such as the Foreign Military Sales Trust Fund, Foreign Service Pension funds
and sundry agency trust funds which have permanent budget authority. The
President's gross budget estimates for these accounts, not including offsetting receipts, by function are as follows:

Function		Budget Authority	Outlays
150	–	$14,310,734,000	$11,308,695,000
600	–	399,749,000	221,511,000
370	–	11,352,000	10,883,000

   The executive branch has submitted no request to alter these funds nor
does the Committee contemplate any legislation which would affect their status.
Therefore, the First Concurrent Budget Resolution should assume the President's
estimates for these budget accounts.

4. Programs Under Committee Oversight Jurisdiction

   Under the Rules of the House, Committee has oversight jurisdiction
over the multilateral development banks and the Export-Import bank. The
President's FY 1983 budget request for these programs is $1.5 billion and
$2.7 billion respectively. The budget resolution should assume the necessary
budget authority and outlays to fulfill the budget request.

5. Credit Programs Under Committee Jurisdiction

   FMS Credits and Loan Guarantees - The President's FY 1983 budget
request contains two types of FMS financing: (1) on-budget direct FMS
credits of $1.739 billion; and (2) off-budget loan guarantees of $3.928
billion for a combined total FY 1983 FMS credit financing program of
$5.668 billion.

   For FY 1983, the current authorization level is $800 million FMS direct
credits, on-budget and $3,269.525 million FMS loan guarantees, off-budget.
The existing authorization levels for the FMS financing program will serve
as the base from which the Committee will give serious consideration to
the President's request for additional on-budget and off-budget FMS financing.

   Overseas Private Investment Corporation (OPIC) - OPIC encourages the
participation of U.S. private capital and skills in the economic and social
development of less-developed friendly countries. Its primary programs are:
(1) political risk insurance against losses due to expropriation, incon-

vertibility, and war damage; and (2) investment financing through loans
and loan guarantees. OPIC operates on a self-sustaining basis and, as such
will have an estimated negative outlay impact on the Federal Budget of
$77.7 million in FY 1983. The executive branch has requested no legislative
changes in OPIC's authorities.

Housing Guaranty Program - The Housing Guaranty Program was established
by the Foreign Assistance Act of 1961 and significantly expanded and altered
in 1965, 1969, 1975, and 1978. The program, consolidated into a single
worldwide authority in 1978, extends guaranties to assist developing countries
in formulating and executing sound housing and community development policies
that meet the needs of lower income groups. Activities to be carried out
will emphasize: (1) sites and services and core housing projects providing
homesites and shelter for poor families; (2) slum upgrading projects
designed to conserve and improve existing shelter; (3) low-income shelter
projects designed for demonstration or institution building purposes; and
(4) project-related community facilities and services. The program will
have an estimated outlay impact of $1.9 million in FY 1983. The executive
branch has requested no legislative changes in this authority.

Attached is a table which lists those programs in the President's
budget which fall under the Committee's authorization jurisdiction. The
table shows the FY 1982 authorization and appropriation levels for each
such program, the FY 1983 authorization levels, the CBO FY 1983 baselines,
the President's FY 1983 budget requests, and the Committee's recommended
levels for FY 1983.

Thank you for your consideration.

With best wishes, I am

                                        Sincerely yours,

                                        Chairman

CJZ:bbeh

attachment

BUDGET PROJECTIONS AND ECONOMIC ASSUMPTIONS

TABLE C-1

THE EFFECT ON BUDGET PROJECTIONS OF SELECTED CHANGES IN ECONOMIC ASSUMPTIONS (By fiscal year, in billions of dollars)

	1983	1984	1985	1986	1987
Real Growth: Effect of One-Percentage-Point Lower Annual Rate Beginning January 1983					
Change in revenues	-9	-23	-35	-45	-60
Change in outlays	2	5	11	17	24
Change in deficit	10	28	46	62	83
Unemployment: Effect of One-Percentage-Point Higher Annual Rate Beginning January 1983					
Change in revenues	-20	-29	-26	-22	-20
Change in outlays	5	10	13	15	17
Change in deficit	25	39	39	37	37
Inflation: Effect of One-Percentage-Point Higher Annual Rate Beginning January 1983					
Change in revenues	6	15	23	32	40
Change in outlays	a	1	5	8	11
Change in deficit	-6	-14	-18	-24	-29
Interest Rates: Effect of One-Percentage-Point Higher Annual Rates Beginning January 1983					
Change in revenues	1	1	1	2	2
Change in outlays	2	6	9	12	14
Change in deficit	1	5	8	10	12

NOTE: Detail may not add to totals because of rounding.

a   Less than $500 million.

Reprinted from U.S. Congress, Congressional Budget Office, *The Economic and Budget Outlook* (Washington, D.C.: Government Printing Office, 1982), table B-1, p. 89.

FUNCTIONAL CATEGORIES OF THE FEDERAL BUDGET

Both the president's budget and congressional budget resolutions list programs by "functional categories." These functions are designed to classify government activities by purpose, regardless of which agencies carry out those activities. As a result, the programs of one department may be spread over several budget functions.

This appendix briefly describes each of the nineteen budget functions and lists the major programs, departments, and agencies.

BUDGET FUNCTIONS

Number	Title
050	National Defense
150	International Affairs
250	General Science, Space, and Technology
270	Energy
300	Natural Resources and Environment
350	Agriculture
370	Commerce and Housing Credit
400	Transportation
450	Community and Regional Development
500	Education, Training, Employment, and Social Services
550	Health
600	Income Security
700	Veterans Benefits and Services
750	Administration of Justice
800	General Government
850	General Purpose Fiscal Assistance
900	Net Interest
920	Allowances
950	Undistributed Offsetting Receipts

FUNCTION 050: National Defense

Funds in this function are provided to develop, maintain, and equip the military forces of the United States, and to finance defense-related activities of the Department of Energy. Major areas of funding include pay and benefits to active military and civilian personnel; military retired pay; research, development, and procurement of weapons systems and supporting equipment; military construction, including family housing; and operations and maintenance of the defense establishment. Funding also is provided for the development and procurement of nuclear weapons and naval reactors.

Major Federal Programs
  Department of Defense—Military
  Atomic Energy Defense Activities
  Defense-related Activities

Major Federal Departments and Agencies
  Department of Defense
  Department of Energy (nuclear weapons and naval reactors)

FUNCTION 150: International Affairs

Funds in this function are provided to finance the foreign affairs establishment, including embassies and other diplomatic missions abroad; loans and technical assistance activities in the less developed countries; security supporting assistance and military assistance to foreign governments; foreign military sales made through the trust fund; U.S. contributions to international financial institutions; and Export-Import Bank activities.

Major Federal Programs
  Foreign Affairs
  Foreign Aid
  Food for Peace
  Security Assistance
  Foreign Military Sales
  Export Promotion
  U.S. Contributions to International Financial Institutions

Major Federal Departments and Agencies
  Department of State
  Department of Defense

Department of the Treasury
Department of Agriculture
Agency for International Development
International Communication Agency
Export-Import Bank of the United States

FUNCTION 250: General Science, Space, and Technology

This function includes space research and technology, general science, and basic research not specifically covered by other functional areas. It represents nearly 20 percent of total federal research and development outlays and includes budgets for the National Science Foundation, certain research programs of the Energy Department, a small Smithsonian Institution program, and nonaeronautical programs of the National Aeronautics and Space Administration (NASA).

Major Federal Programs
General Science and Basic Research
Space Research, Technology, and Applications

Major Federal Departments and Agencies
Department of Energy
National Science Foundation
National Aeronautics and Space Administration

FUNCTION 270: Energy

This function represents a consolidation of nearly all federal energy and energy-related programs.

Major Federal Programs
Energy Supply
Energy Research, Development, and Demonstration
Energy Conservation
Strategic Petroleum Reserve
Nuclear Regulation
Tennessee Valley Authority Power Program
Synthetic Fuels Program
Energy Information, Policy, and Regulation Programs

Major Federal Departments and Agencies
  Department of Energy
  Nuclear Regulatory Commission
  Tennessee Valley Authority

FUNCTION 300: Natural Resources and Environment

Programs in this function are designed primarily to develop, manage, and maintain the nation's natural resources and environment.

Major Federal Programs
  Natural Resources Management, Development, and Conservation
  Water Resources Programs
  Management and Acquisition of Natural Parks
  Sewage Treatment Plant Construction Grant Programs
  Implementation of National Environmental Program
  Development, Regulation, and Conservation of Minerals
  Management and Preservation of the Public Lands

Major Federal Departments and Agencies
  Department of the Interior
  Department of Agriculture
  Department of Commerce
  Army Corps of Engineers
  Environmental Protection Agency

FUNCTION 350: Agriculture

Programs in this function are designed to assist food purchasers, provide market information and services, and support food research. Food producers are assisted through deficiency payments, disaster payments, product purchases, insurance, nonresource loans, and regular loans. Market information and services include Department of Agriculture administration, animal disease prevention, distribution of market information, and numerous regulatory activities. Research provides for direct support of federal biological research facilities, grants for state-supported facilities, and economic analysis.

Major Federal Programs
  Price Support and Related Programs (Commodity Credit
      Corporation)
  Federal Crop Insurance

Farmers Home Administration (FmHA)
Farm Loans
Research Programs
Extension Programs
Consumer Protection, Marketing, and Regulatory Programs
Economic Intelligence

Major Federal Departments and Agencies
Department of Agriculture

FUNCTION 370: Commerce and Housing Credit

This function is highly volatile from year to year because of changing economic conditions. It provides for assistance through the government's unsubsidized housing programs and other activities related to commerce and finance.

Major Federal Programs
Mortgage Insurance Programs
Secondary-market Support for Insured Mortgages
Rural Housing Programs
Payments to the Postal Service
Small Business Loan and Guarantee Assistance
Thrift and Deposit Insurance
Regulatory Agencies

Major Federal Departments and Agencies
Department of Housing and Urban Development: Federal Housing
Administration (FHA) and Government National Mortgage
Association (GNMA)
Department of Agriculture: Farmer Home Administration (FmHA)
Postal Service
Small Business Administration
Regulatory Commissions
Federal Deposit Insurance Corporation and Similar Agencies

FUNCTION 400: Transportation

This function provides assistance for transportation activities, including ground (highway, railroads, and mass transportation), air, and water transportation programs. The transportation function includes major grants-in-aid programs to support state and local activities.

Major Federal Programs
  Highway Construction and Safety
  Mass Transit
  Railroad Assistance
  Airways and Airports
  Maritime Subsidies
  Coast Guard

Major Federal Departments and Agencies
  Department of Transportation
  Department of Commerce
  NASA: Aeronautical Research
  Interstate Commerce Commission
  Civil Aeronautics Board

FUNCTION 450: Community and Regional Development

Community development block grants account for about half of the outlays in this function. The balance is composed of a wide variety of small urban and rural development grant programs and disaster and emergency aid programs.

Major Federal Programs
  Community Development Block Grants
  Urban Development Action Grants
  Rehabilitation Loans
  Rural Development Assistance
  Economic Development Assistance
  Appalachian and Other Regional Programs
  Indian Programs
  Disaster Relief and Small Business Administration (SBA) Disaster
     Loan Programs
  Flood Insurance

Major Federal Departments and Agencies
  Department of Housing and Urban Development
  Department of Agriculture: Farmers Home Loan Administration
  Department of Commerce: Economic Development Administration
  Department of Interior: Bureau of Indian Affairs
  Small Business Administration

FUNCTION 500: Education, Training, Employment, and Social Services

This function includes programs designed to promote the general extension of knowledge and skills and to help individuals become self-supporting members of society: child development, elementary, secondary, vocational, and higher education programs; employment and training and public service employment programs; and grants to states for general social and rehabilitation services. Funds in this function may be made available as income support directly related to training or education; cash payments (scholarship, loans, or stipends) to persons to enable them to participate in education or training programs; grants to states, local governments, Indian tribes, or public and private institutions to operate local educational, employment, training, or social service programs; and direct research and departmental management expenditures.

Major Federal Programs
  Financial Assistance for Elementary and Secondary Education
    (ESEA)
  Occupational, Vocational, and Adult Education
  Higher Education Student Assistance
  Higher Continuing Education
  Grants to States for Social and Child Welfare Services
  Human Development Services

Major Federal Departments
  Department of Education
  Department of Health and Human Services
  Department of Labor
  Office of Personnel Management
  Community Services Administration, ACTION, and Various Other
    Independent Agencies

FUNCTION 550: Health

The major purpose of programs in this function is to promote the physical and mental health of the population. Programs include financing of medical care for aged, poor, and disabled persons; provisions of health care for certain population groups, such as American Indians and merchant seamen; and grants to states, localities, and community groups to support health services programs. The function also includes research into the causes and cures of disease; promotion of consumer and occupational health and safety; training support for health workers and researchers; construction of health training and health-care facilities; and food, drug, and other product safety and inspection programs.

Major Federal Programs
  Health Insurance for the Aged and Disabled (Medicare)
  Grants to States for Medical Assistance Programs (Medicaid)
  National Institutes of Health
  Alcoholism, Drug Abuse, and Mental Health Research, Training, and Services
  Health Resources Development
  Disease Prevention and Control

Major Federal Departments and Agencies
  Department of Health and Human Services
  Department of Labor
  Office of Personnel Management
  Department of Agriculture: Food Safety and Quality Service

FUNCTION 600: Income Security

Programs in this function provide cash and in-kind benefits to persons who need permanent or temporary income assistance. More than half of the estimated outlays will go to retirees through such programs as Social Security, federal civilian retirement, and railroad retirement. In-kind assistance benefits include Food Stamps and other food programs, as well as subsidized housing. Cash assistance benefits include Aid to Families with Dependent Children (AFDC) and Supplemental Security Income (SSI); and special benefits for disabled are provided through special programs, the largest of which is the disability component of Social Security. Finally, unemployment benefits are included.

Major Federal Programs
  Old-Age, Survivors, and Disability Insurance
  Railroad Retirement
  Special Benefits for Disabled Coal Miners
  Federal Employee Retirement and Disability
  Unemployment Compensation
  Trade Adjustment Assistance
  Supplemental Security Income (SSI)
  Grants to States for Maintenance Payments (primarily AFDC)

Housing Assistance
Food Stamps
Child Nutrition

Major Federal Departments and Agencies
  Office of Personnel Management
  Department of Agriculture: Food and Nutrition Service
  Department of Health and Human Services
  Department of Housing and Urban Development
  Department of Labor
  Railroad Retirement Board
  Department of State

FUNCTION 700: Veterans Benefits and Services

Most programs in this function are administered by the Veterans Administration in support of former members of the armed services and their survivors and dependents. More than half of the outlays in this function are for income security programs: compensation, pensions, and life insurance. Nearly one-third of the outlays are targeted for hospital and medical care for veterans, and about one-tenth for veterans education, training, and rehabilitation. Housing and other benefits constitute the remainder. Nearly the entire function requires current action by Congress, yet the bulk of these outlays is virtually uncontrollable because of the entitlement nature of the major programs.

Major Federal Programs
  Veterans Disability Compensation
  Veterans Pensions
  Veterans Education and Training (G.I. Bill)
  Veterans Hospital and Medical Care
  Veterans Guaranteed Housing Loans
  Veterans Life Insurance

Major Departments and Agencies
  Veterans Administration

FUNCTION 750: Administration of Justice

The largest law enforcement program in this function are for the operations of the Federal Bureau of Investigation, Customs Service, and Immigration and Naturalization Service. The balance of the function is made up of various federal activities in law enforcement, prosecution, correctional activities, and the judiciary.

Major Federal Programs
  Federal Bureau of Investigation
  Drug Enforcement
  Immigration and Naturalization
  Legal Services
  Customs
  Prisons
  Courts
  Law Enforcement Assistance
  Juvenile Delinquency Prevention

Major Departments and Agencies
  Department of Justice
  Department of the Treasury
  Civil Rights Commission
  Legal Services Corporation

FUNCTION 800: General Government

This function covers the general overhead costs of the federal government. By far the largest proportion of new budget authority and outlays is attributed to operations of the Treasury Department (including the Internal Revenue Service). The balance is distributed among a large number of relatively small accounts. The legislative branch typically accounts for about one-fifth of the net total.

Major Federal Programs
  Legislative Branch Activities
  Federal Buildings Fund
  Income Tax Administration

Major Departments and Agencies
  Congress and its Agencies
  Executive Office of the President
  Department of the Treasury
  General Services Administration
  Office of Personnel Management
  Department of Interior, Office of Territories

FUNCTION 850: General Purpose Fiscal Assistance

The General Revenue Sharing program accounts for nealy 90 percent of this function. The balance is composed of antirecession assistance, payments and loans to the District of Columbia, and portions of certain taxes and other charges returned to states and local governments.

Major Federal Programs
General Revenue Sharing
Antirecession Assistance
District of Columbia Federal Payment
Payments in Lieu of Taxes

Major Departments and Agencies
Department of the Treasury
Department of the Interior

FUNCTION 900: Net Interest

This function is composed almost exclusively of interest on the public debt, to which is added amounts of interest paid by the federal government (interest on income tax refunds, for example) and from which are deducted offsetting receipts, such as interest paid by the Federal Financing Bank on behalf of its Treasury borrowings. The Treasury Department accordingly accounts for almost all of the transactions in this function.

Major Federal Program
Interest on the Public Debt
Interest on Income Tax Refunds
Interest Received by Certain Trust Funds

Major Departments and Agencies
Department of the Treasury

FUNCTION 920: Allowances

Allowances include estimates for civilian agency pay increases and contingencies to cover anticipated expenditures not included in the accounts of any executive agency.

Major Federal Program
   Civilian Agency Pay Raise
   Contingencies for Other Requirements

FUNCTION 950: Undistributed Offsetting Receipts

Undistributed offsetting receipts involve financial transactions that are deducted from budget authority and outlays of the government as a whole. The three items in this function are the employer share of employee retirement funds; rents and royalties from oil leases on the Outer Continental Shelf; and receipts from federal surplus property disposition.

MEMBERS OF THE HOUSE AND SENATE BUDGET COMMITTEES

HOUSE BUDGET COMMITTEE

Democrats   *Telephone*

James Jones (Okla.) 225-2211
Jim Wright (Tex.) 225-5071
Stephen Solarz (N.Y.) 225-2361
Timothy Wirth (Colo.) 225-2161
Leon Panetta (Calif.) 225-2861
Richard Gephardt (Mo.) 225-2671
Bill Nelson (Fla.) 225-3671
Les Aspin (Wis.) 225-3031
Bill Hefner (N.C.) 225-3715
Thomas Downey (N.Y.) 225-3335
Brian Donnelly (Mass.) 225-3215
Mike Lowry (Wash.) 225-3106
Butler Derrick (S.C.) 225-5301
George Miller (Calif.) 225-2095
William Gray, III (Pa.) 225-4001
Pat Williams (Mont.) 225-3211
Geraldine Ferraro (N.Y.) 225-3965
Howard Wolpe (Mich.) 225-5011
Martin Frost (Tex.) 225-3605
Vic Fazio (Calif.) 225-5716

Republicans

Delbert Latta (Ohio) 225-6405
Bud Shuster (Pa.) 225-2431
Bill Frenzel (Minn.) 225-2871
Jack Kemp (N.Y.) 225-5265
Ed Bethune (Ark.) 225-2506

Lynn Martin (Ill.) 225-5676
Bobbi Fiedler (Calif.) 225-5811
Tom Loeffler (Tex.) 225-4236
Bill Gradison (Ohio) 225-3164
Connie Mack (Fla.) 225-2536

SENATE BUDGET COMMITTEE

Republicans   *Telephone*

Pete Domenici (N. Mex.) 224-6621
William Armstrong (Colo.) 224-5941
Nancy Landon Kassebaum (Kans.) 224-4774
Rudy Boschwitz (Minn.) 224-5641
Orrin Hatch (Utah) 224-5251
John Tower (Tex.) 224-2934
Mark Andrews (N. Dak.) 224-2043
Steven Symms (Idaho) 224-6142
Charles Grassley (Iowa) 224-3744
Bob Kasten (Wis.) 224-5323
Dan Quayle (Ind.) 224-5623
Slade Gorton (Wash.) 224-2621

Democrats

Lawton Chiles (Fla.) 224-5274
Ernest Hollings (S.C.) 224-6121
Joseph Biden, Jr. (Del.) 224-5042
J. Bennett Johnson (La.) 224-5824
Jim Sasser (Tenn.) 224-3344
Gary Hart (Colo.) 224-5852
Howard Metzenbaum (Ohio) 224-2315
Donald Riegle, Jr. (Mich.) 224-4822
Daniel Patrick Moynihan (N.Y.) 224-4451
J. James Exon (Nebr.) 224-4224

NOTES

Notes to Chapter 1

1. The reasons for this dual requirement are mostly political. For a good discussion of how this process came to be, see Allen Schick, *Congress and Money: Budgeting, Spending and Taxing* (Washington, D.C.: The Urban Institute, 1980).

2. A further explanation of how to read and analyze the various tables in each of the budget documents provided to Congress by the president can be found in part 2 of this book.

3. Theoretically, if the federal government stopped all new spending, budget authority and outlays could be reconciled so that they would equal each other. To do this, however, budget authority that was unused for some reason (unspent appropriations, rescissions, etc.) also would have to be taken into account.

4. U.S. Congress, Congressional Budget Office, *The Economic and Budget Outlook* (Washington, D.C.: Government Printing Office, 1982), p. 88.

Notes to Chapter 2

1. See chapter 1 for an explanation of authorizations and appropriations.

2. A "supplemental appropriation" is an act appropriating funds in addition to the regular annual appropriation. Supplemental appropriations ordinarily are enacted when the need for additional funds is too urgent to be postponed until the next regular appropriation is considered. In some cases a supplemental appropriation is used to lower the requested amount in the annual appropriation.

3. Appendix D provides a description of each budget function, including a list of the major agencies, departments, and programs each contains. See chapter 1 for an explanation of budget functions.

4. A "point of order" is a formal contention by a representative or senator that the pending legislation violates the Constitution, rules, or precedents, and, therefore, no longer should be considered. In this case the violation would be

of the Budget Act. If a point of order is made against a spending or revenue bill because it violates the second resolution, and it is sustained, the bill will be withdrawn from further consideration.

5. In 1982 Congress did not even bother to pass a second resolution. Instead, a provision was included in the first resolution that automatically made it the second resolution when Congress did not pass a regular second resolution by October 1. In 1982 Congress decided not to make any revisions in the fiscal policy and spending revenue totals of the first resolution even though there was a widespread agreement that the economic assumptions on which it was based were no longer valid.

6. The only other experiences with reconciliation, in 1980 and 1981, also occurred in the first resolution. To date, reconciliation has never occurred in the second resolution, as it was intended.

7. U.S. Congress, Committee on the Budget, House of Representatives, *The Congressional Budget Process: A General Explanation* (Washington, D.C.: Government Printing Office, 1981), p. 17.

Notes to Chapter 3

1. William Greider, "The Education of David Stockman," *The Atlantic Monthly*, December 1981, pp. 27–54.

2. For further information on the executive budget process, see Aaron Wildavsky, *The Politics of the Budgetary Process* (Boston, Massachusetts: Little, Brown and Company, 1979).

3. The exact sequence of events was as follows: January 15, 1981—submission of Carter fiscal 1982 budget proposal; January 20—President Reagan sworn into office; February 18—Reagan economic plan presented in general terms to joint session of Congress; March 10—detailed Reagan budget revisions to Carter proposal submitted to Congress; April 7—additional details on Reagan budget submitted to Congress.

4. The CBO report actually is required to be submitted by April 1. However, CBO generally has provided its report by mid-March so that it is available to the Budget Committees before their consideration of the first concurrent resolution.

5. The Joint Economic Committee is required to submit a report recommending fiscal policies that should be appropriate to achieve the goals of the Employment Act of 1946, as amended.

Notes to Chapter 4

1. Appendix A is a copy of the first budget resolution for fiscal 1983.

2. Appendix D provides a description of the 19 budget functions, including a list of the major programs in each. See chapter 1 for an explanation of budget functions.

3. The informal procedures are, of course, continual. The staffers of the budget and other committees meet regularly to compare spending estimates and to discuss and negotiate possible violations of the Budget Act.

4. The current policy baseline is the level of spending that would occur if this year's programs simply were continued at the same level next year. Most programs are adjusted for inflation. See the glossary for a more complete definition.

5. The years following the budget being considered are referred to as the "out years." The figures shown for those years are not the final proposals, only the spending that would occur in those years if the proposed budget were accepted, no further changes were passed, and if the economy behaved in the way assumed in the budget.

6. See chapter 14 for a full description and discussion of the credit budget.

7. Allen Schick, *Congress and Money* (Washington, D.C.: The Urban Institute, 1980), p. 263.

8. Each functional presentation included a narrative discussion that did explain the different options in somewhat more detail. But the discussions were only about one paragraph long and left many questions about specific programs unanswered.

9. For example, any amendment that seeks to increase the budget authority and outlays for one function also would have to specify the additions to the aggregate totals of budget authority and outlays, and would have to adjust the surplus/deficit accordingly. Likewise, an amendment to lower the deficit would have to specify the functional decreases that would constitute that change.

10. For example, if function 850: General Purpose Fiscal Assistance had been changed previously by an amendment that dealt only with it, a second amendment to increase or decrease the function would not be in order unless it also included changes in another function.

11. This refers to section 302(A) of the Congressional Budget and Impoundment Control Act, Public Law 93-344.

Notes to Chapter 5

1. See chapter 1 for an explanation of the difference between an authorization and an appropriation.

2. See the glossary for a complete definition of continuing resolutions.

3. See the glossary for a complete definition of tax expenditures.

4. Appendix B contains the fiscal 1983 March 15 reports from the House Armed Services and Foreign Affairs Committees.

Notes to Chapter 6

1. Section 7 of the resolution provided as follows:

> If Congress has not completed action by October 1, 1982, on the Concurrent Resolution on the Budget required to be reported under section 310(A) of the Budget Act for the 1983 fiscal year, then, for purposes of section 311 of such Act, and section 4 of this resolution, this concurrent resolution shall be deemed to be the concurrent resolution required to be reported under section 310(A) of such Act.

See appendix A for a copy of the fiscal 1983 first budget resolution.

2. Any provision of the Budget Act can be avoided if Congress agrees to waive it for the consideration of a bill. The procedure in each house is different. In the Senate, the waiver must be agreed to by unanimous consent during floor debate on the bill. In the House, the waiver must be passed as part of the rule which allows the bill to be considered.

Notes to Chapter 7

1. The Budget Act actually does not specify "increases" or "decreases" but rather "changes." Therefore, reconciliation also could be used to require a spending increase or revenue decrease.

2. Appendix A is the first budget resolution for fiscal 1983. Section 2 is the reconciliations instructions.

3. Reconciliation can be accomplished either through a bill or a joint resolution.

4. In the House, the Rules Committee would have to request that the Budget Committee make those changes. In the Senate, a motion would have to pass during debate on the reconciliation bill that would send the bill back (recommit) to committee with instructions on how the changes were to be accomplished. In theory, this motion could be made by a member of the Budget Committee.

5. Two examples of nonbudget provisions from the fiscal 1982 reconciliation bill are the inclusion by the House Energy and Commerce Committee of a repeal of several provisions of the Powerplant and Industrial Fuel Use Act, and the Senate Commerce, Science, and Transportation Committee's inclusion of several major changes in the Communications Act.

Notes to Chapter 8

1. Louis Fisher, *Presidential Spending Power* (Princeton, New Jersey: Princeton University Press, 1975), p. 158.

2. Ibid., p. 148.

3. The president also is required to publish the deferral or rescission message in the *Federal Register* and to submit a cumulative report to both houses each month on the rescissions and deferrals proposed to date that year.

Notes to Chapter 10

1. Appendix D provides a description of the 19 budget functions, including a list of the major programs. Chapter 1 contains a complete explanation of budget functions.

2. See the glossary for a definition of constant and current dollars.

3. See chapter 1 and appendix D of this book.

Note to Chapter 11

1. See chapter 8 for an explanation of rescissions. See the glossary for a definition of supplemental appropriations, off-budget federal entities, government-sponsored enterprises, and advance funding.

Notes to Chapter 14

1. The Budget Act actually requires that these estimates be provided in November before the budget is submitted to Congress. By mutual agreement of the House and Senate Budget and Appropriations Committees, the Joint Economic Committee, and OMB, they are now provided with the rest of the budget when it is submitted to Congress.

2. Office of Management and Budget, *Special Analyses, Budget of the United States Government, Fiscal Year 1984* (Washington, D.C.: Government Printing Office, 1983), "Current Services Estimates," p. 4.

3. *Special Analyses,* "Current Services Estimates," p. 4.

4. See chapter 1 for a discussion and explanation of economic assumptions.

5. See chapter 8 for an explanation of rescissions and deferrals.

6. Appendix D provides a description of the 19 budget functions, including a list of the major programs in each. Chapter 1 contains a complete explanation of budget functions.

7. See the glossary for an explanation of off-budget agencies and government-sponsored enterprises.

8. Ibid.

GLOSSARY

Advance funding Budget authority provided in an appropriation act that allows funds to be committed to a specific purpose (obligated) and spent during this fiscal year even though the appropriation actually is for the next fiscal year. Advance funding generally is used to avoid requests for supplemental appropriations for entitlement programs late in a fiscal year when the appropriations for the current fiscal year are too low.

Aggregates The totals relating to the whole budget rather than a particular function, program, or line item. The five budget aggregates are budget authority, outlays, revenues, deficit/surplus, and level of public debt.

Appropriation An act of Congress that allows federal agencies to incur obligations and make payments from the Treasury for specified purposes. An appropriation is the most common means of providing budget authority and usually follows the passage of an authorization. (See chapter 1.)

Authorization An act of Congress that establishes or continues a federal program or agency either for a specified period of time or indefinitely; specifies its general goals and conduct; and usually sets a ceiling on the amount of budget authority that can be provided in an appropriation. An authorization for an agency or program usually is required before an appropriation for that same agency or program can be passed. (See chapter 1.)

Authorization committee A standing committee of the House or Senate with legislative jurisdiction over the subject matter of those laws that establish or continue the operations of federal programs or agencies. An authorization committee also has jurisdiction in those instances when spending authority is provided in the substantive legislation. (See *Backdoor authority*.)

Backdoor authority or **backdoor spending**   Budget authority provided without the passage of an appropriation. The most common forms of backdoor authority are borrowing authority, contract authority, and entitlements. Permanent appropriations that continue without any current congressional action also are considered to be backdoor spending.

Balanced budget   When revenues equal outlays.

Baseline   A projection of the federal revenues and spending that would occur if current laws and policies were to continue unchanged. This projection is not a forecast of a future federal budget. It is only a benchmark against which proposed changes in taxes or spending programs can be measured. The baseline concept is used interchangeably with current policy and current services.

Block grant   See *Grant*.

Borrowing authority   A form of budget authority that permits a federal agency (other than the Treasury and Federal Financing Bank) to borrow funds from the public or another federal fund or account and to incur obligations and make payments of specifed purposes out of that borrowed money. Borrowing authority differs from an appropriation, which permits a federal agency to incur obligations and make payments directly from the Treasury. Borrowing authority is a type of backdoor spending. (See *Backdoor authority or backdoor spending*.)

Budget authority   The authority granted to a federal agency in an appropriations bill to enter into commitments that result in immediate or future spending. In most cases budget authority is not the amount of money an agency or department actually will spend during a fiscal year but merely the upper limit on the amount of new spending commitments it can make. The three basic types of budget authority are appropriations, borrowing authority, and contract authority.

Categorical grant   See *Grant*.

Concurrent resolution on the budget   Legislation passed by both houses of Congress that establishes, reaffirms, or revises the congressional budget for a fiscal year. The first concurrent resolution, which is expected to pass by May 15, is the congressional budget in its earliest form. This resolution establishes targets for the aggregate levels of budget authority, outlays, revenues, and deficit or surplus, the appropriate level of the public debt, and an estimate of the budget authority and outlays for each of the nineteen budget functions. The second concurrent resolution, which is expected to pass by September 15, revises or reaffirms the aggregate and functional targets of the first resolution and changes the aggregates into an

absolute "ceiling" on spending and a minumum "floor" on revenues. If needed, subsequent budget resolutions for a fiscal year may
be adopted at any time after the passage of the second resolution.
A concurrent budget resolution does not require the president's
signature to become law.

Congressional budget   The budget established by Congress in a concurrent resolution on the budget.

Constant dollars   The dollar value of goods and services adjusted for
inflation. Constant dollars are determined by dividing current dollars by an appropriate price index, a process generally known as
"deflating." Constant dollars are used to discount increases or decreases in prices when comparing transactions over a period of
time.

Contract authority   A type of budget authority that permits a federal
agency to incur obligations before appropriations have been passed
or in excess of the amount of money in a revolving fund. Contract
authority must be funded subsequently by an appropriation so that
the commitments entered into can be paid.

Controllability   The ability to increase or decrease spending for a particular program in the fiscal year in question. "Relatively uncontrollable" refers to spending that will occur without any new action
by Congress and usually refers to spending that results from entitlements and other open-ended programs, permanent appropriations, and commitments now coming due from budget authority
enacted in prior years.

Credit budget   A presentation of all credit programs that are conducted
by the federal government, regardless of whether they formally are
included in the unified budget. It includes all new credit activities
of the federal government on a gross basis: on-budget direct loans,
off-budget direct loans, and loan guarantees. It does not include
the credit activities of government-sponsored enterprises. The credit
budget records all credit activities at the point of obligation or
commitment for credit, rather than at the point when the loans
actually are made, because the obligation level is the point at which
Congress can exert control.

Crosswalk   A procedure for translating budget information from one
form to another—for example, from a budget resolution to an authorization or appropriations bill.

Current dollars   The dollar value of a good or service in terms of the
prices at the time the good or service was sold.

Current policy   An estimate, provided by the Congressional Budget
Office, of the budget authority and outlays needed for a program
or agency to continue to operate this year at the same level as in

the past year, adjusted for inflation, including anticipated changes in the number of beneficiaries, and changes already enacted in law.

Current services   An estimate, provided each year by the Office of Management and Budget in *Special Analysis A*, of the budget authority and outlays that would be needed in the next fiscal year to continue federal programs at their current levels. These estimates reflect the anticipated costs of continuing these programs at their present spending levels without any policy changes, that is, ignoring all new presidential and congressional initiatives that have not yet been enacted into law. (See chapter 14.)

Deferral   An action of the president that temporarily withholds, delays, or precludes the obligation or expenditure of budget authority. A deferral must be reported by the president to Congress in a deferral message. The deferral can be overturned if either house passes a resolution disapproving it. A deferral may not extend beyond the end of the fiscal year in which the message reporting it is transmitted to Congress. (See also *Impoundments, Rescission.*)

Deficit   When outlays exceed revenues.

Economic assumption   Estimates of how the national economy will behave. The three main economic assumptions that affect the budget are unemployment, inflation, and growth in the gross national product (GNP). (See chapter 1.)

Entitlement   Legislation that requires the payment of benefits to all persons or governments that meet the eligibility requirements established in the law. Examples of entitlement programs are Social Security, Medicare, and veterans pensions. (See also *Backdoor authority* and *Controllability.*)

Expenditures   Actual spending, generally interchangeable with outlays.

First concurrent resolution on the budget   See *Concurrent resolution on the budget.*

Fiscal policy   Federal policies on taxes, spending, and debt management, intended to promote the nation's goals, particularly with respect to employment, gross national product, inflation, and balance of payments. The budget process is a major vehicle for determining and implementing fiscal policy.

Fiscal year   Any yearly accounting period. The fiscal year for the federal government begins on October 1 and ends on September 30. The federal fiscal year is designated by the calendar year in which it ends; for example, fiscal 1983 begins on October 1, 1982, and ends on September 30, 1983.

Forward funding   Budget authority provided in an appropriations act that allows funds to be committed to a specific purpose (obligated) this year for programs that will be implemented next year. Forward funding often is used for education programs, so that grants can be made by the federal government before the start of the school year, and local school officials can plan their budgets.

Full funding   Providing the budget authority to cover the total cost of a program or project at the time it first is approved. This differs from partial or incremental funding, where budget authority is provided only for those obligations of the program or project that are likely to be incurred in a given fiscal year.

Function or functional classification   The system of presenting budget authority, outlays, and tax expenditures in terms of the principal purposes the programs are intended to serve. Each program is placed in the single functional category that best represents its major purpose, regardless of the department that administers it. Both the president's budget and the congressional budget resolutions are presented primarily by function. (See chapter 1.)

Government-sponsored enterprises   Enterprises that are established and chartered by the federal government to perform specific functions under the supervision of a government agency. As private corporations, these enterprises are excluded from the budget. Examples of government-sponsored enterprises are the Federal Home Loan Bank Board and the Federal National Mortgage Association.

Grant   A cash award given by the federal government to a state or local government or other recipient for a specified purpose. This differs from a grant-in-aid, which is a grant limited solely to a state or local government. The two major forms of federal grants are "block" and "categorical." Block grants are awarded primarily to general purpose governments, are distributed to them according to the formulas established in the law, and can be used for any locally determined activities that fall within the functional purpose of the grant as stated in the law. Categorical grants can be used only for a specific purpose and usually are limited to narrowly defined activities.

Grants-in-aid   For the purposes of the budget, grants-in-aid consist of federal outlays used to support, promote, or encourage specific state and local government activities.

Impoundment   An action by the president that prevents the obligation or expenditure of budget authority. Deferrals and rescissions are the two types of presidential impoundments. (See chapter 8.)

Loan guarantee   An agreement by which the government pledges to pay part or all of the principal and interest of a loan to the lender or holder of a security if the borrower defaults. If it becomes necessary for the government to pay part or all of the loan principal or interest, the payment is an outlay. If not, then the loan guarantee does not affect federal spending and appears in the budget only as budget authority.

Midyear review of the budget   An updated version of the president's original budget proposal, prepared by the Office of Management and Budget and required to be submitted to Congress by July 15. The midyear review includes revised projections on the economy and its likely effect on the president's program, any policy changes proposed by the president since the budget was submitted, and the latest information on the previous year's spending and revenue totals.

Obligated balance   The amount of a budget authority committed for a specified purpose but not yet actually spent.

Obligational authority   The total available to an agency in a given fiscal year. Obligational authority is the sum of the budget authority newly provided in a fiscal year, the balance of budget authority from prior years that has not yet been obligated, and amounts authorized to be credited to a specific fund or account during that year, including transfers between accounts.

Obligations   Spending commitments by the federal government that will require outlays either immediately or at some point in the future.

Off-budget agencies   Certain federally owned and controlled agencies that have been excluded from the unified budget by law. The budget authority and outlays for these agencies are not, therefore, included in the totals for the budget. The outlays of off-budget agencies, when added to the unified budget deficit, comprise the total government deficit that has to be financed by borrowing. Examples of off-budget agencies include the Postal Service and the Federal Financing Bank.

Office of Management and Budget (OMB)   The division of the Executive Office of the President that assists the president in the discharge of her or his budgetary and management responsibilities.

Offsetting receipts   Money collected by the federal government that is deducted from budget authority and outlays because it comes from market-oriented government activities or intragovernmental transactions. Offsetting receipts usually are displayed in the function in which they occur and are deducted from the functional or agency budget authority and outlays. (See also *Undistributed offsetting receipts.*)

Outlays   The actual amount of dollars spent for a particular activity. The total results from both new budget authority provided this year and from unexpended balances of budget authority provided in previous years. It is the level of outlays compared to the level of revenues that determines whether the budget is in surplus or deficit.

President's budget   The proposal sent by the president to Congress each year as required by the Budget and Accounting Act of 1921, as amended. The president's budget consists of five documents: *Budget of the United States Government; Budget of the United States Government, Appendix; Special Analyses, Budget of the United States Government; The United States Budget In Brief;* and *Major Themes and Additional Budget Details.* (See chapters 9–14.)

Program   An organized set of activities directed toward a common purpose or goal, undertaken or proposed by an agency to carry out its responsibilities.

Reconciliation   The process used by Congress to force its committees to comply with the fiscal policy of a budget resolution. (See chapter 7.)

Rescission   An action of the president that cancels budget authority previously appropriated but not yet obligated or spent. A proposed rescission must be reported to Congress by the president in a rescission message. If both houses do not approve of the proposed rescission within forty-five days, the president must obligate the budget authority as it was intended by Congress.

Revenues   Money collected by the federal government as duties, taxes, or as premiums from social insurance programs.

Second concurrent resolution on the budget   See *Concurrent resolution on the budget.*

Spending committees   The standing committees of the House and Senate with jurisdiction over legislation that permits the obligation of funds. For most programs, the House and Senate Appropriations Committees are the spending committees. For other programs, the authorization legislation permits the obligation of funds without an appropriation, and so the authorization committees have the spending power. The revenue-raising committees (House Ways and Means and Senate Finance) at times also can be considered to be spending committees because of tax expenditures.

Supplemental appropriations   An act appropriating funds as an addition to the regular annual appropriation. Supplemental appropriations generally are enacted when the need for additional funds is too urgent to be postponed until the next regular appropriation is considered.

Surplus   The amount by which revenues exceed outlays.

Tax expenditures   Losses of tax revenues that result from federal tax law permitting special exclusions, exemptions, deductions, credits, preferential tax rates, or deferred tax liability.

Total obligation authority (TOA)   See *Obligational authority.*

Transition quarter (TQ)   The three-month period between the end of fiscal 1976 and the beginning of fiscal 1977 (July 1 to September 30, 1976) resulting from the change from a July 1 through June 30 federal fiscal year to an October 1 through September 30 fiscal year.

Trust funds   Federal funds collected and used to carry out specific purposes and programs under trust agreements or statutes, such as Social Security and unemployment trust funds. Trust funds cannot be used for purposes other than those for which they originally were intended.

Undistributed offsetting receipts   Money collected by the federal government from payments to trust funds by government agencies for their employees' retirement, interest paid to trust funds on their investments in government securities, and proprietary receipts from rents and royalties on the Outer Continental Shelf. These receipts are not distributed to the function which best describes their substantive role but are included as a separate function.

Unexpended balance   The amount of budget authority previously granted to an agency but still unspent and available for future spending. The unexpended balance is equal to the sum of the obligated and unobligated balances.

Unified budget   The present form of the budget of the federal government in which receipts and outlays from federal funds and trust funds are consolidated into a single document.

Unobligated balance   The amount of budget authority previously granted to an agency but not yet committed by that agency that continues to be available for commitment in the future.

These definitions have been adapted, in part, from U.S. General Accounting Office, *A Glossary of Terms Used in the Federal Budget Process*, Third Edition, Report No. PAD-81-27 (Washington, D.C.: Government Printing Office, March 1981).

INDEX

narrative statement of program and
performance, 82
National Defense function, see
function
national income accounts, 78
national needs, 65, 70, 71
Natural Resources and Environment
function, see function
Net Interest function, see function
Nixon, Richard, 15, 57

object classification schedules, 82–
83
obligated balance, 152
obligational authority, 152
obligations, 58, 77, 152
off-budget federal entities, 79, 86,
152
Office of Management and Budget
(OMB), 14, 17, 23, 24, 25, 59, 63,
86, 145, 152
offsetting receipts, 152
OMB, see Office of Management and
Budget
operating expenses, 98
outlays, 2–5, 16, 29, 37, 43, 65, 74,
76, 98, 152–153

permanent appropriations, see
appropriations
personnel summary, 84
Pierce, Samuel, 24
point of order, 18, 141–142
Postal Service, U.S., 86
Powerplant and Industrial Fuel Use
Act, 144
presidential budget, 13, 14, 15–16,
17, 23–28, 45, 153
presidential veto, 17, 48, 57
program, 8, 153
program and financing schedule, 80–
81
public debt, 16, 30, 37
Public Law, 93-344, see Congressional Budget and Impoundment
Control Act

Reagan, Ronald, 19, 23, 24, 25, 46,
54–55, 59, 142

reconciliation, 15, 18, 19, 50, 51, 53–
56, 112–116, 142, 144, 153
Research and Development, 64, 93,
100
rescissions, 20–21, 57–60, 79, 86,
94, 141, 144, 153
revenue floor, 18, 19, 49, 50, 54
revenues, 7, 16, 30, 37, 153
Rules Committee, House, 42, 56, 144
Rural Electrification Administration,
86
Rural Telephone Bank, 86

salaries, 4
Schick, Allen, 141, 143
schedules of permanent positions,
84–85
scorekeeping, 47
second concurrent resolution on the
budget, see concurrent resolution
on the budget
Section 302 allocations, 43, 47
Social Security, 2
*Special Analyses, Budget of the
United States Government*, see
also the individual analysis, 64,
93–102
spending ceiling, 18, 19, 49, 50, 54,
55
spending committees, 153
spending priority, 13, 15, 23, 29, 48,
49, 53, 54
spendout rates, 4, 50
SPR Petroleum Account, 86
Stockman, David, 24
Student Loan Marketing Association,
86
subfunction, see function
supplemental appropriations, see
appropriations
surplus, 14, 16, 30, 37, 154

targets, 16, 45, 54, 55
tax committees, 30
tax expenditures, 47, 65, 154
Tax Expenditures, 93, 99
third concurrent resolution on the
budget, see concurrent resolution
on the budget